HIGHER REALISM

A NEW FOREIGN POLICY
FOR THE UNITED STATES

SEYOM BROWN

PARADIGM PUBLISHERS

Boulder & London

green press INITIATIVE

P... ...ed to preserving ancient forests and natural resources. We elected to print this title on 30%
p... ...rocessed chlorine free. As a result, for this printing, we have saved:

   5 Trees (40' tall and 6-8" diameter)
   1,962 Gallons of Wastewater
   4 million BTU's of Total Energy
   252 Pounds of Solid Waste
   473 Pounds of Greenhouse Gases

F... ... s paper choice because our printer, Thomson-Shore, Inc., is a member of Green Press
I... ... dedicated to supporting authors, publishers, and suppliers in their efforts to reduce their
use ... ...dangered forests.

For more information, visit www.greenpressinitiative.org

Environmental impact estimates were made using the Environmental Defense Paper Calculator. For more information visit: www.papercalculator.org.

For Vanda

Copyright © 2009 Paradigm Publishers

Published in the United States by Paradigm Publishers, 3360 Mitchell Lane, Suite E, Boulder, CO 80301 USA.

Paradigm Publishers is the trade name of Birkenkamp & Company, LLC, Dean Birkenkamp, President and Publisher.

Library of Congress Cataloging-in-Publication Data

Brown, Seyom.
  Higher realism : a new foreign policy for the United States / Seyom Brown.
    p. cm.
  Includes bibliographical references and index.
  ISBN 978-1-59451-398-5 (hardcover : alk. paper)
  1. United States—Foreign relations—Philosophy. 2. United States—Foreign relations—21st century. I. Title.
  JZ1480.B68 2009
  327.73001—dc22

                2008039249

Printed and bound in the United States of America on acid-free paper that meets the standards of the American National Standard for Permanence of Paper for Printed Library Materials.

Designed and Typeset by Straight Creek Bookmakers.

13 12 11 10 09   1 2 3 4 5

Contents

Preface

A comprehensive new foreign policy for the United States—formulated by an individual. "Higher Realism," no less. What can justify such a seemingly presumptuous enterprise?

Precisely because U.S. foreign policy now involves so many specialized domains, each with its own dilemmas and politically charged controversies, often requiring technical knowledge, attempts to freshly formulate a comprehensive design for the country's role in the world can rarely get out of committee, so to speak. And if they do, the result is unlikely to move much beyond BOMFOG (Brotherhood of Man/Fatherhood of God) verities. Yet without a coherent view of how the various policy domains crucially affect, and can be at tension with, each other, and without a set of ordering principles for determining priorities and trade-offs, even the purposefully practical recommendations of diverse-membership groups (such as the foreign policy planks in the platforms of the political parties) are likely to run off madly in all directions.

There are times when it is appropriate that consistency and coherence give way to "politics" in the policy formulation process—so as to ensure that competing special interests are adequately represented and that there will be accountability to affected communities. Ultimately, broad popular support is a requisite for a sustainable foreign policy, and it is a component of the national and world interests that I argue must be served. But this is one of those times when a systematic dialogue among policy makers, analysts, and the informed and attentive public is required on the needs and values of the nation as a *whole* and how these might be realized in the evolving global system. My proposal for a new foreign policy is designed to stimulate that systematic dialogue.

Neither I, nor any other individual, has anywhere near the required expertise in all of the fields encompassed by the new foreign policy I am advocating. In many of these domains, those of us aspiring to provide the needed synthesis therefore must rely on trusted "brokers" for understanding the complexities and assessing the comparative advantages and disadvantages of contending policies. This has certainly been true in my effort.

Mentors early in my professional career whose lasting impact on my thinking deserves acknowledgment include Hans J. Morgenthau, Robert Endicott Osgood, Morton A. Kaplan, Tang Tsou, and Leo Strauss (my graduate professors at the University of Chicago); Alexander L. George, Bernard Brodie, Albert Wohlstetter, and James Schlesinger (my senior colleagues at the RAND Corporation); Herman Kahn (that much-maligned and much-misunderstood strategic guru, whom I nicknamed Maherman Khandi); and Richard Falk.

Midcourse on the trajectory toward Higher Realism, I received important feedback and guidance from policy analysts and policy makers Paul Warnke, William Bundy, Leslie Gelb, Morton Halperin, Tony Lake, Zbigniew Brzezinski, Marshall Shulman, Marshall Goldman, Henry Owen, Joseph Nye, James Chase, Alton Frye, Jerome Kahan, Barry Blechman, Fred Bergsten, Lester Brown, Thomas Hughes, Edith Brown Weiss, and Larry Fabian.

More recently, when I was working on my Brookings book *The Illusion of Control,* crucial reality checks were provided by Richard Haass, James Steinberg, and Michael O'Hanlon. During this period the President of Brookings, Strobe Talbott, and I began a dialogue, carried on since then, on alternative visions (and dilemmas) of global governance.

While I was engaged in the actual writing of *Higher Realism,* invaluable perspectives were provided by Graham Allison, Steven Miller, Sean Lynn-Jones, Richard Rosecrance, Stephen Walt, Kevin Ryan, and other colleagues at Harvard University's Belfer Center for Science and

International Affairs, where as a senior fellow I was provided a stimulating venue for working on and testing out some of the core ideas. As senior advisor to the Security Studies Program of the Massachusetts Institute of Technology, I also received senior advice on geopolitical realities and military policy from Carl Kaysen, Barry Posen, and Harvey Sapolsky. Other colleagues with whom I had useful exchanges on issues I was developing in the book are Stanley Hoffmann, Robert Keohane, Robert Hunter, Lawrence Finkelstein, Robert Paarlberg, Owen Cote, Jr., John Hamre, Larry Korb, Robert Pastor, Kenneth Oye, Anthony Lake, Robert Gallucci, Robert Einhorn, Andrew Bacevich, Vanda Felbab-Brown, Walter Russell Mead, William Zartman, Robert Litwak, Elliot Feldman, Lily Gardner Feldman, Ramchandra Guha, Jessica Tuchman Mathews, Robert Art, Cindy Williams, Chris Preble, Steven Clemons, Michael Lind, William Ruger, Robert Jordan, James Hollifield, Schuyler Marshall, Donald Hays, Matthew Elias, Emile Sahliyeh, Michael Desch, Eugene Gholz, Joshua Itzkowitz-Shifrinson, and Sanjeev Kumar.

As this is a policy-prescriptive book, not an academic treatise, the endnote citations do not detail the ways each of these colleagues (and probably some I have left out) has informed and helped shape my analysis. And some of them, I know, as they now read the final product, may well take issue not only with specific parts of the argument but with its general thrust; yet I acknowledge them nonetheless as valued interlocutors.

Many of those mentioned have been devotees of Realism, what I call Conventional Realism. My effort to persuade them as well as general readers to embrace a somewhat enlarged and visionary foreign policy called Higher Realism may seem to imply that their worldview is inferior to the worldview I am offering. I do argue that Higher Realism provides a more appropriate paradigm for the emergent realities, but, as I elaborate in the text, the "Higher" is meant to describe added dimensions of analysis and focus, not to trump Conventional Realism with a mere term. For to do the latter would be to invite a fatuous verbal dual in which Higher Realism is caricatured as "far out," " spacey," or "in orbit." I do like the metaphor of viewing Planet Earth from outer space (as shown on the dust jacket of this book); but it should be noted that the reconnaissance satellites that give us such inspiring images are also capable of high-resolution photography that can focus in with remarkable precision on particular terrestrial symptoms—such as the melting of glaciers, desertification, encampments of homeless refuges, provocative missile tests—of emerging fundamental threats to human security and well-being.

My invitation to policy makers, scholars, and the attentive public is to devise and support a U.S. foreign policy fully responsive to the increasingly evident incongruence between the radically growing material integration of the world's peoples and their persisting political and cultural diversity. Higher Realism, as defined and elaborated in the text, provides the parameters of such a policy—for cooperatively bringing about greater congruence between the material and political/cultural spheres in ways that do not create a backlash against the United States for pretensions of omnipotence and omniscience.

This admittedly ambitious project would never have materialized in the form of a readable book were it not for the attentive editorial guidance provided by Jennifer Knerr and Melanie Stafford of Paradigm Publishers. The counsel I received from Jennifer and her staff throughout the project is reflective of the appropriateness of the imprimatur of this young, high-quality press. I am complimented and proud to have Higher Realism appear in their line of titles.

Finally, a note of special appreciation to my most valued colleague: my wife, Vanda Felbab-Brown. Even though busy with her own important research and writing projects, Vanda's keen and informed critical assessments of the arguments I have been developing have been indispensible in my effort to make sure that the second term in the book's title is merited. My words of deep affection for her are classified.

Seyom Brown

A U.S. Foreign Policy
of Higher Realism

T he country is at a historic juncture where its leaders must be willing to sacrifice immediate popularity in order to serve fundamental national interests that supersede party or factional interests. This requires thoroughgoing review and reconceptualization of the country's national interests, a continuing determination of priorities and trade-offs among them in response to emerging opportunities and threats, and the resolve to implement appropriate policies that may be highly controversial. Ultimately, the people will approve or disapprove, but their consent to, or reservations about, the country's new foreign policy must be informed by a comprehensive and deeply probing analysis at the highest levels.

I offer here a contribution to the kind of deliberation that is required. It involves some corrective analysis to disenthrall ourselves from the still-persisting delusions of superpowerism. Most important, and the main thrust of this book, is the reformulation of the U.S. role and obligations in the emerging world system—a foreign policy I call *Higher Realism.*

Realism means more than being consistent with material and social realities (who wouldn't make such a claim?). In the U.S. foreign policy community—among policymakers, analysts, and scholars—the way of thinking called Realism holds that, given the absence of a world system of enforceable law and order, the United States must depend ultimately on its own power to maintain the security and well-being of the nation.

Conventional Realists thus support a power-oriented and unabashedly self-interested foreign policy. The high card in the game of international power politics is one's military capabilities, and the "self" is the United States. Moreover, the security of the whole country, the well-being of the whole country—the national interests—are given priority over local, class, or other special interests.

The foreign policy I propose embraces these core premises as necessary, yet woefully insufficient, for determining how the United States should respond to the international threats and opportunities ahead. *Higher Realism* rectifies the deficits in Conventional Realism not only by enlarging the traditional concept of power to include noncoercive (or what Joseph Nye calls "soft power") components[1] but also by giving high priority to *world* interests that have become inseparable from the country's national interests. Higher Realism does not assume that what is good for the United States is, by definition, good for the world. But it does recognize that, more and more, what is good for the world *is* good for the United States.

Some of the world interests (economists call them international "public goods") such as preventing developments that could jeopardize the healthy survival of the human species—a nuclear World War III or drastic changes in the planet's climate—are clearly also essential to the security and well-being of the people of the United States. Others, such as a well-functioning and basically free global market and unimpeded worldwide lines of transportation and communication, are highly important for U.S. prosperity. Still others, such as the alleviation of poverty and disease and the advancement of human rights, are crucial for the avoidance of state failure and market failure in countries in which the United States has large strategic or economic stakes. Moreover, poverty, disease, and political oppression, even in countries of little strategic or economic weight themselves, are producing the hordes of stateless refugees and migrants that other countries (including the United States) are finding it difficult to absorb without destabilizing political, economic, or social consequences. And finally, Higher Realism recognizes that, for both pragmatic and moral reasons, the United States should be promoting processes and institutions of international accountability—binding on itself as well as others—for actions (or inaction) that have major impact across borders.

Thus, Higher Realism transcends the conventional dichotomies of realism versus idealism and self-interest versus altruistic morality. It points to U.S. foreign policy centered on cooperation with others in serving international public goods and world interests on which the security and well-being of each nation ultimately depends. Opinion surveys show that most people in the United States will support and are willing to contribute toward programs around the world to help those in need, insofar as this does not undermine their own security and well-being. Most people seek ways of making their own lives better without depriving others of a better life. Most people want to be treated fairly and also to treat others fairly. They recognize there are often difficult trade-offs to be made among policies serving nearby and distant interests and among programs of immediate impact and those that could fundamentally affect the lives of future generations. And they respect policymakers willing to grapple with the hard choices forthrightly.

The book is forward-looking. I have no intention of adding to the bookshelves and computer archives already crowded with indictments of the Bush foreign policy. But an initial clearing away of the fantasies and fallacies responsible for the serious mistakes of recent administrations (including Bill Clinton's) is required for a clearheaded understanding of the international opportunities and difficulties facing the United States in the years ahead.

This introductory chapter first previews my critique of the arrogance in U.S. foreign policy since the end of the Cold War and my explanation of why Conventional Realism provides an inadequate corrective. The rest of the chapter summarizes the essential features of Higher Realism and its major policy implications. It also provides a guide to

3

the subsequent chapters, where the analysis and prescriptions will be presented in greater detail.

The Pax Americana Delusion

The fantasy that the United States is both omnipotent and omniscient— all-powerful after the Soviet Union opted out of the Cold War and all-knowing with respect to the economic and political systems under which people should live—still lingers among foreign policy influentials in both political parties. This hubristic delusion hangs on in many quarters despite its tragic consequences in Iraq (and possibly yet in Afghanistan) and the unprecedented global backlash against other U.S. policies. Conventional Realists are saying "we told you" that the world-transforming ambitions of the Clinton administration and the post-9/11 Bush administration violated the first rule of prudential statecraft: the country's commitments should not exceed its capabilities.

But for the true believers in an American mission to help transform the world into a global society of peaceful democracies, the solution is not to reduce our commitments; it is to enhance our capabilities.

The corollary tendency to divide the world into good guys versus bad guys—the former being champions of free markets and democracy and the latter, if they resort to violence, being "terrorists"—is also quite alive. And insofar as it continues to pervade Washington's public diplomacy, it will continue to validate charges that the U.S. government is hypocritical and mendacious when alliances of convenience with dictators and perpetrators of brutality, plus its own violations of human rights in the name of the war on terrorism, contradict the righteous rhetoric.

From Unipolarity to Polyarchy

The Pax Americana delusion was reinforced by the belief among many geopolitically oriented policymakers and analysts (some of whom were nonideological Realists) that the world, no longer "bipolar," was now basically "unipolar." Most countries and peoples, even if temporarily opposed to particular U.S. policies, would ultimately gravitate into the superpower's orbit. There were debates over whether U.S. primacy was attributable mainly to "hard power" (its military and economic clout) or "soft power" (basically, the attractiveness of its way of life), and what should be the proper mix of the two in U.S. foreign policy. Unipolarity, however, at least up until key U.S. allies objected to Operation Iraqi Freedom, was widely regarded as the self-evident geopolitical reality. And neo-Wilsonians and neoconservatives alike, despite the former's championing of multilateral institutions, acted and spoke as if a unipolar Pax Americana were a normative good.

But the gap between the promise of a unipolar Pax Americana and its performance has been enormous, embarrassing its former proponents in the United States and those around the world who were persuaded to jump onto Washington's post–Cold War bandwagon. True, the United States remains the most influential single actor in the global system. Its cooperation or opposition can often determine the fate of policies and programs of others around the world. But as became evident with the U.S. failure to gain UN Security Council backing for Operation Iraqi Freedom, being the only superpower is not the same as having implementable hegemony over all others in the system.

The false promise of unipolar peace and the increasing resistance to U.S. hegemonic assertiveness have prompted analysts and statespersons to revive the concept of *multi*polarity for comprehending and responding to the emergent complexities. Comprising a number of great powers, each one the dominant country in its region, multipolarity has been widely assumed to be the normal condition of the international system.

Standard histories of politics among the great powers show that if one of them attempts aggressively to lord it over the rest, others will form a coalition against the would-be continental or global hegemon—the fate of France under Napoleon Bonaparte in the late eighteenth and early nineteenth centuries and of Germany under Adolph Hitler in the twentieth century. From this perspective, both unipolarity and bipolarity (the latter occurring when countries attempt to "balance" or put down the unipolar pretensions of an imperial power) are temporary abnormalities.

President Nixon, advised by Henry Kissinger, who had written his doctoral dissertation on post-Napoleonic European multipolarity, forecast the reemergence of multipolarity in a post–Cold War world. The emerging system would be run essentially by the United States, Russia, China, Japan, and the European Community—each pursuing its own interests in a five-sided balance of power. And today, in reacting to Washington's pressures to get them to conform to U.S. policy preferences, high officials in Moscow, Beijing, Tokyo, Delhi, Paris, and other European capitals are wont to remind their U.S. counterparts that we are living in a "multipolar world."

The problem with the multipolar model, both as a descriptor of contemporary world politics and as a guide for grand strategy, is its lack of correspondence to the structural realities and to the way states and other actors in the system are behaving. None of the big five (or six or seven) is capable of exercising the degree of control over its neighbors to warrant being regarded as the region's polar power, and any such pretension of regional hegemony would be resisted by its neighbors. Which country in Asia, for example—China, Japan, India—can claim, or will allow its rivals to claim, the mantle of the region's polar power? Even in subregions—say, Southeast Asia—neither Indonesia nor Vietnam, nor Thailand nor Malaysia, nor the Philippines (forget Australia)—is inclined to grant primacy to the others. Rather, each of them as well as the smaller states in the region, determined to ensure their ability to control their own affairs and to maximize their bargaining power vis-à-vis the larger states, has been diversifying its active international relationships in trade, investments, technological cooperation, and mutual security arrangements. This pattern of diversifying one's (inter)dependent relationships, as opposed to consolidating a bilateral relationship or alliance with a particular benefactor, is characteristic of today's international politics around the globe—in Central Asia, in the Middle East, in Africa, in the Americas, and in Europe.

The diversification of dependency, the diffusion of power, and the multidimensionality of power have dissipated the magnetic pull that either global or regional hegemons require to sustain unipolarity or multipolarity. As a result, hardly any countries are unidirectionally aligned in their major international relationships. Allies on one issue (for example, strengthening international policing against terrorism) may be adversaries on others (for example, the right of self-determination for ethnic minorities or the location of pipelines for transporting Eurasian oil); today's partner may be tomorrow's rival and vice versa, depending on the issue at hand. Neither unipolar nor multipolar, the emergent global system is not so much anarchic as it is *poly*archic.[2]

The Polyarchy comprises nation-states, subnational groups, transnational special interests, and religious and ethnic communities along with regional and global multilateral institutions, some with supranational powers. The members of various of these entities are simultaneously members of some of the other entities, which are often in competition with each other for resources and loyalty on the part of their constituents. The resulting cross-pressures on countries, political movements, and peoples can have both positive and negative effects on U.S. and world interests.

Positively, the polyarchic cross-pressures make it difficult to whip up the total nation-versus-nation hostility, class conflict, and religious-sectarian hatred that lead to major war and violent conflict of genocidal proportion. Negatively, the cross-pressures and the volatility of alignments and antagonisms make it difficult to put together and sustain multilateral collective action to provide the international public goods that world and U.S. interests demand. It is especially for the purpose of generating the amount of global community commitment required to overcome the inhibitors of the needed collective action that a new U.S. foreign policy must be formulated—a foreign policy realistically responsive to the complexities of the emergent Polyarchy, yet dedicated to achieving that higher level of international collaboration the world once again is looking for the United States to join in sponsoring.

7

Realism: Conventional and Higher

Realism holds that the cardinal purpose of U.S. foreign policy is to serve the country's irreducible national interests—as stipulated in the preamble to the U.S. Constitution: "to establish justice, to insure domestic tranquility, to provide for the common defense, and to secure the blessings of liberty to ourselves and our posterity." In this first imperative, both Conventional and Higher Realism are in accord. They are also in accord in favoring a statecraft of bargaining rather than hegemonic diktat, yet backed up by military power sufficient to deter military actions against the United States and efforts to physically deny access to foreign sources of essential energy supplies.

Moreover, both Conventional and Higher Realism counsel that the United States, although still the most powerful country, should use its power prudently. It should not engage in hubristic attempts to run the world. Nor should it intervene militarily in other countries unless required to secure the irreducible U.S. national interests or, under broad international mandate, to prevent genocide or comparable gross violations of elemental human security.

The central problem with Conventional Realism is that it is long on what the United States should *not* attempt to do yet short on what should be done to counteract the chaos in the Polyarchy that inhibits needed cooperation in the provision of international public goods. Conventional Realism views the world as essentially stymied when it comes to preventing the spread of weapons of mass destruction, effectively countering global warming, and alleviating the starvation of billions of people. Nor does Conventional Realism have a vision of system transformation, let alone global governance, for ameliorating the looming dangers.

Higher Realism at its very core embraces the fact that the irreducible national interests have become inextricably bound up with world interests—with the security and well-being of people all around the globe—and that the citizens of the United States of America will be unable to "secure the blessings of liberty to ourselves and our posterity" unless the government recasts its foreign policy to be consistent with the evolving global system.

But the evolving system, the Polyarchy (many rulers) of states and powerful nonstate actors with shifting alignments and antagonisms, is incapable of generating international action vital to the physical safety, health, and well-being of the people of the United States and the world without a new explosion of international cooperative activity. The needed cooperation dwarfs even the burst of international cooperation that followed the end of World War II. It will take a variety of institutional forms—regional, functionally specific, many outside of the UN system. But once again, it requires active and central participation by the United States. Absent significant U.S. participation in the cooperative provision of crucial global public goods in the fields of conflict control, the economy, and the environment, the evolving Polyarchy could well degenerate worldwide into a condition of raw anarchy in which in far too many places (including in the United States) life will be nasty, brutish, and short.

Higher Realism does share the premise of various other schools of Realism, and of Realpolitik statecraft, that foreign policy must give priority to the interests of the whole country over special or parochial interests. But it transcends exclusively nationalistic definitions of self-interest, recognizing that the health and well-being of one's own country are crucially connected, albeit often indirectly, with the health and well-being of people around the world. Higher Realism also transcends the immediate here and now—looking toward the long-term effects of current action (or *in*action)—programming the impact on future generations into the evaluation of current policy choices.

Higher Realism shares as well Conventional Realism's understanding that, particularly in the absence of strong institutions of global governance, U.S. foreign policy must be centrally concerned with the country's international *power*—its resources and instruments for realizing its purposes—especially when opposed by others. It agrees with Conventional Realism that U.S. statecraft must be directed first and foremost at ensuring that others do not impose their will on the United

States. Accordingly, the military and economic instruments of power, and the will to invoke them coercively at times, must remain essential components of U.S. grand strategy. But Higher Realism also appreciates the crucial importance of subjecting the coercive application of U.S. material power to widely accepted standards of legitimacy and, if possible, broad international authorization.

A rigidly nationalistic, blatantly materialistic, and amoral Realism plants the seeds of its own obstruction—stimulating others from whom the country requires cooperation even for the realization of its narrow self-interests to mobilize against it. Moreover, there are large and well-organized domestic political constituencies that want and expect the United States to serve broader world community interests, especially the resolution of internationally destabilizing conflict and the alleviation of the suffering of those in situations of grinding poverty or subject to brutal repression. These constituencies and their representatives in high office want their country to pursue policies that are "right"—that is, morally meritorious in serving the well-being of others and refraining from the infliction of avoidable harm on them. Such altruism is not incompatible with Realism, certainly not with Higher Realism; it need not undermine the primacy of the country's economic and strategic self-interests. Rather, the quest is for policy options that can simultaneously secure self-interest and the well-being of others. Public opinion surveys show that there is broad support inside and outside of government for the United States to do good while doing well.

Yet, ironically, a visible post-Iraq role for the United States of promoting peace, justice, basic economic security, and human rights around the globe risks being seen as another hubristic self-appointed mission. And it will be quixotic—unless the United States adapts to the fact that the world's contemporary cultural and political diversity is an inherent legacy of millennia of human history and is justifiably resistant to homogenization into any one sociopolitical or economic way of life. Higher Realism, though broadly supportive of democracy and human rights, therefore opposes the view that a universal adoption of the essential features of the U.S. market economy and democratic polity or even more broadly

"Western" modernization—however desirable for some societies—is necessary for world order and justice.

Higher Realism does, however, insist on the necessity of the universal enhancement of norms and institutions of international accountability. It takes issue with the tendency of Conventional Realists (neo- or classical) to discount international norms and institutions as mere "epiphenomenal" expressions of underlying power realities. Higher Realism regards strengthened international accountability among countries and other entities that can seriously affect one another—even if at times constraining the United States from acting with complete flexibility—as a world interest increasingly crucial to the long-term security and well-being of the people of the United States.

World Interests: Concept and Content

The concept of world interests, like the concept of national interests, derives from the understanding that for any society, some conditions are required for the effective functioning of that society as a *whole* and for the well-being of most of its members. These—at least these—are its interests. Whether the society is a microsociety, like a family or clan, a village, or a tribe, or whether it is a city, metrocomplex, agroindustrial locality, nation, multinational regional community, or the entire global society of countries, the society's very existence presumes a degree of crucial interdependence and interaction among its members. At best, there will be mutual commitment to promote one another's well-being; at worst, the interdependence can lead to internecine warfare.

When members of a society morally embrace the fact of their interdependence and foster norms of mutual accountability and responsibility, the society becomes a community. In a genuine community, there will be some institutionalization of mutual accountability and responsibility and some reliable means of providing for community "public goods": the care of natural resources and ecologies essential to the community's well-being, infrastructures of communication and transportation, a workable economic system for exchanging goods and services, at least a rudimentary system for peacefully resolving disputes among members, and the ability to protect the community arrangements and structures against destructive attacks. These norms and structures of mutual commitment are what distinguish a community from a mere society. They are the community's interests, its vital interests, if you will.

Although the terms *world community* and *international community* are frequently used, global society as a whole still falls far short of being a community. It is a society with an increasing amount of interdependence, and with some regional and functional community arrangements, but not really a comprehensive community. Yet even in its condition as a society (and putative community), the world does have some basic—yes, vital—interests that must be tended to in order to avoid a host of looming threats to the security and well-being of much of humankind—including the people of the United States.

Here then, by way of brief introduction, are the *world* interests—the interests of world society (still not a community)—that need to be asserted, elaborated, and implemented by its members. Singly and in combination these interests and the policies required to serve them (often involving difficult trade-offs) are an essential part of a U.S. foreign policy of Higher Realism, for, as will be demonstrated more conclusively in subsequent chapters, they are indeed in the national interest of the United States.

Ensuring the Healthy Survival of the Human Species

The sine qua non of all the other world and national interests is the survival of humankind in a healthy condition—which can no longer be taken for granted given the mass-destruction capabilities in the possession of powerful actors and the capacity of humans, even when acting with peaceful intent, to drastically alter the natural environment. The preservation of planetary conditions necessary for healthy human survival has come to require substantial strengthening of global arms-control regimes—particularly for Weapons of Mass Destruction (WMD). This will involve a substantial increase in resources for detecting and arresting the proliferation of WMD and their components. And it may involve considerably more limitations on U.S. WMD capabilities—actual and potential—than Washington now accepts.

The human species as a whole is not yet threatened by projected levels of global warming. Different regions and communities may experience more or less disruption over the coming decades, and some communities may even benefit from a rise in agricultural productivity. But over the long run, if not reversed, global warming and other threats to important ecological conditions could progressively impact other world interests in ways that might cumulatively jeopardize the well-being of most of humankind. The range of the planet's environmental vulnerabilities merits serious concern, and *Higher Realism* gives efforts to deal with the impending problems special attention as a world interest.

Reducing the Role of Force in World Politics

This interest requires new exemplary leadership from the United States, which requires backing off from its own force-centered diplomacy, dispensing with the rhetoric of military preemption and preventive war, and adopting a posture of military restraint. The demilitarization of diplomacy should be reinforced by a credible pledge to avoid applying large-scale lethal force except as a last resort, and then only if nonmilitary means clearly appear unable to avoid even more horrendous death and destruction than are likely to be produced by the contemplated war. In addition, fresh policy initiatives are needed to regulate or shut down global arms bazaars, licit and illicit, of conventional weapons as well as of WMD components. Moreover, a central aspect of the de-emphasis of force-centered diplomacy is the enhancement of international security institutions and processes that privilege conflict de-escalation— for example, mediation and provision of positive conflict-resolution incentives—over deterrence and defense. Resorting to military force along with employing coercive deterrent and compelling strategies and capabilities must, of course, remain in the toolbox of U.S. foreign policy, but they should be held in reserve as instruments of control against those who have violated the norms of peaceful bargaining—not waved around as everyday tools of diplomacy.

Alleviating Poverty and Disease

The world's affluent countries and peoples cannot be adequately insulated (physically and psychologically) from indirect and direct effects of the abject poverty now suffered by some 20 percent of humanity. Even those among us with no transnational altruistic sensibility need to be concerned about the politically and economically destabilizing impact of tens of millions of homeless refugees from improverished regions and failing states. The conditions from which they are escaping and the conditions in the refugee camps into which they are temporarily crowded are breeding grounds for contagious diseases such as tuberculosis, HIV/AIDS, and SARS, which are then spread within the more affluent societies into which the refugees migrate. Accordingly, the United States, even if only for the well-being of its own people, should take on the obligation to share the burden more equitably than it has been doing of alleviating the widespread destitution.

Maintaining a Well-Functioning Global Economy

A breakdown or substantial constriction in the global economic system, with its basically free exchange of goods, services, and money, would severely threaten both the nongovernmental and governmental sectors of the U.S. economy and polity, since so much of the buying, selling, and investing engaged in by the people of this country has a foreign client or label of origin. The global free market, which it is largely in U.S. interests to sustain, nevertheless requires considerable regulation of and compromises with total economic freedom lest the uneven distribution of its benefits among countries and economic sectors within countries generate protectionist reactions. Trade-constricting and investment-constricting backlashes by uncompetitive countries and political pressures within globally active economies for import restrictions to shield sectors unable to compete with cheap goods produced in countries with low factor costs (especially low wages and few health and safety regulations) could provoke competitive raising of trade barriers and currency manipulations that could bring on severe recessions and even a global depression. In other words, the normal behavior of the international economy and the normal patterns of domestic politics are inadequate to the essential task of maintaining a well-functioning global market. The important world and U.S. interests in avoiding a retrogression to a "beggar thy neighbor" international economy will require energetic and creative economic policymaking in the years ahead.

Arresting Disturbances to Vital Ecologies

Although the failure to sustain the planet's moderate climate and to preserve other important ecological relationships around the world may not directly produce a net decline in the U.S. economy as a whole (for example, the melting of Arctic ice can open up the polar region for more petroleum exploitation), widespread disruption of local economies and habitats, even as others prosper, will negatively affect the conflict control and global poverty alleviation interests. And over the long run, the ecological consequences could also threaten the healthy survival of the human species. From this perspective, the currently observable increase in the average temperature of the planet can pose serious threats to the United States. The dominant scientific consensus supports the urgency of proactive programs to arrest global warming before it reaches an irreversible tipping point. It is no exaggeration to say that there is a vital national as well as world interest in the development of alternative (non-CO_2-emitting) energy sources, along with agreements binding on at least the largest producers of greenhouse gases (the United States, China, and India) to drastically reduce their carbon emissions over the coming decades. The cluster of conflict control, poverty alleviation, and environmental interests also gives urgency to dedicated U.S. participation in international and domestic initiatives to counter depletion and/or abuse of other essential ecological resources: species biodiversity, water, forests, fertile land, wildlife, the atmosphere, and outer space.

Promoting Democracy and Human Rights

Although aware of the controversies over their appropriate forms in different societies, Higher Realism affirms that political systems based on the informed consent of the governed that are respectful of fundamental human rights—democracy in its fullest sense—are in the world interest. The information revolution and the inability of governments to hide their repressive policies have been disruptive of world order situations in which consent-of-the-governed principles and basic human rights are blatantly violated. But the United States, if its efforts on behalf of democracy and human rights are again to be regarded as anything but hypocritical, needs to urgently correct its own questionable practices, which, in the name of fighting terrorism, have given succor to repressive governments around the world that justify brutal trampling of human rights by citing national security.

Although a world largely composed of democracies might be more peaceful than a world populated by autocracies and dictatorships, one should not fallaciously and dangerously deduce from this proposition that there is a world interest in fomenting insurrections and/or mobilizing military interventions to depose nondemocratic regimes. First of all, not all elected governments are more peaceful externally, even though the historical record shows that they rarely fight each other. There are authoritarian countries—Egypt and Jordan, for example—in which efforts at rapid democratization may lack the cultural and sociological soil to take root, and in which premature electoral democratization may result in majoritarian tyranny that tramples the rights of minorities and individuals—policies supported by the voters and by their representatives in parliament, but tyranny nonetheless. Egypt and Jordan are also examples of authoritarian regimes that are considerably more constructive on Israel-Palestine issues than is the democratically elected Hamas. And although democratization and economic progress do go hand in hand in many developing countries, it is also true that rapid political transformations from authoritarianism to democracy often tend to bring on dangerous levels of domestic instability disruptive of sustained economic growth.

These complicated relationships pose problems when it comes to translating U.S. preferences for a world of democratic states into here-and-now policies. How should states be dealt with that are failing both economically and politically? Should the lives of millions of people in their jurisdictions be further jeopardized by insistence on progress in democratization and human rights as a precondition for giving them economic aid? In response to the extreme of genocide or other gross "crimes against humanity," punitive economic sanctions and military intervention may well be warranted. But in many of these states, democracy and human rights are more likely to take root if implanted by local reformers able to adapt political change to the indigenous culture. Pressures from outsiders, especially Americans today—no matter how well intentioned and knowledgeable—are prone to offend nationalist sensibilities and inadvertently strengthen the hands of those who benefit from the autocratic status quo.

Policymakers should ask, case by case, whether world and U.S. interests and the well-being of the populations directly affected will be better served by giving precedence to an assertive democratization policy or to policies of constructive engagement even with rather unsavory governments. Higher Realism is informed by these complexities. It operates from the premise that the world interest in promoting freedom and democracy is best furthered through such prudential case-by-case assessments—with substantial input from the locals—of feasibility and consequences and of expected costs to other world interests rather than on the basis of a universal strategy of democratization.

Respecting Cultural and Religious Diversity

U.S. preferences for particular kinds of political and economic systems must also be pragmatically constrained by the fundamental reality of a culturally diverse world. And there is ample evidence in the multiplicity of religions that the gods themselves are not in complete agreement on the best design of human communities.

Accordingly, the United States should be generally supportive of efforts by distinct cultural communities around the world to practice their own ways of life, and to devise their own political and economic systems, and it should refrain from intervening to compel them to emulate the U.S. or other "Western" models. In other words, although favoring "freedom," the United States should never be in the business of forcing people to be free as Americans define it. This should not, however, preclude interventions legitimized by a broad international consensus to counter genocide and other crimes against humanity as defined in the statute of the new International Criminal Court. Nor should such forbearance prevent the United States from engaging in internationally authorized peacekeeping or conflict-control operations where required to prevent an eruption of violence.

Fostering Transnational Accountability

All of these world interests imply a greater willingness than in previous historical eras by statespersons, powerful private interests, and the general public around the world to treat the inhabitants of planet Earth as citizens of a global community. But world society cannot be deemed a community unless there is considerable mutual accountability across national borders for how people deal with the planet's resources and for how they treat each other. The accountability principle can be stated simply: those who can or do crucially affect the security or well-being of others (especially by inflicting harm) are answerable to those whom they immediately and directly affect and to the larger society whose well-being, norms, and behavior are implicated. The principle is simple, but its implementation is pervaded by complexities.

Not all of the accountability obligations and processes can operate globally. Some could involve only two or three neighboring states; some—on the model of the European Union—will cover whole regions or continents; and some, such as those required to deal with global warming or the stability of the international monetary system, may have to operate worldwide. The most dependable accountability relationships will be functionally specific—that is, applicable to the unique problems in a particular sector.

Fortunately, there is some rudimentary scaffolding upon which to build in the fields of arms control, counterterrorism, international commerce, international transportation (sea and air), communications, environmental management, and human rights. In each of these realms, states and nongovernmental actors have discovered that "positive sum" benefits can be achieved through institutionalized mutual accountability—even if only establishing predictability in one another's behavior and reducing the costs of fresh negotiations and transactions dispute by dispute. New accountability processes and institutions are needed, however, to deal with the interdependence of developments in the various sectors of world society—for example, trade, transborder ecologies, migration and refugee issues, peace and security, conflict and arms control, and gross violations of the fundamental rights of peoples and persons.

This book has two main objectives. First, I aim to show why, at this particular juncture in the evolution of world society, it is crucial not only for the security and well-being of the people of the United States but also for the healthy survival of the human species that the United States develop and conduct a global policy along the parameters sketched above. Second, I want to provide to public officials, policy analysts, and attentive members of the public whose support will be necessary an illustrative menu of instruments and programs for implementing the basic policy—showing how it merits *both* the Higher (global and beyond the simply materialistic) and Realism (interest-based and politically feasible) terms in the concept.

The Chapters

Chapter 1 describes and analyzes the essential characteristics of the emergent global system within which the United States will have to pursue its security and well-being in the decades ahead. I show why neither unipolarity nor multipolarity is an adequate concept for understanding this emergent configuration of world politics, and how their oversimplification of the geopolitical realities has been at the root of U.S. actions abroad that have undermined basic U.S. interests. I develop the argument that it was the false promise of a unipolar world, with its Pax Americana illusions of omnipotence and omniscience, that produced one of the most embarrassing eras in U.S. foreign policy. I also contend that viewing the world as multipolar is not the appropriate corrective, for the concept inflates the determination of other great powers to mobilize their international friends and clients to "balance" the power of the United States. I show how this "not with us therefore against us" fallacy can become a self-confirming hypothesis, however, as U.S. confrontational rhetoric and posturing in response to those who balk at Washington's initiatives drive even countries who are normally local rivals to coalesce in opposition to such paranoid self-righteousness. The analysis reveals how both the concepts of unipolarity and multipolarity have their source in an overly simple, monotonic notion of the concept of power itself.

The chapter proceeds to describe and analyze the emerging polyarchic system in detail—with its changing kaleidoscope of amity and enmity among the myriad significant actors on the world stage: nation-states, subnational and transnational sectarian and ethnic movements, terrorist networks, criminal syndicates, international and limited supranational institutions, multinational firms, and transnational nongovernmental interest groups and organizations. I show that, characteristically, coalition partners on one issue are opponents on another issue, and today's principal friend may be tomorrow's main adversary. Reliable and durable international alliances and robust multilateral collective security arrangements are difficult to sustain, and the provision of these and other essential international public goods lags seriously behind the growing need for them.

Chapter 2 defines and elaborates the essential features of Higher Realism, a foreign policy designed to respond to the frustrations, dangers, and opportunities in the emergent Polyarchy. The policy is both adaptive and transformative. It recognizes and adapts to the postimperial, postcolonial world of culturally diverse peoples determined to maintain their own ways of life, proud communities who can make it very costly—terrorism being one of the means—for any state or movement that forcibly attempts to homogenize or subordinate them into a polity dominated by a different cultural community. But the new foreign policy is at the same time transformative in its response to the increasingly urgent requirement for new and enhanced forms of international cooperation to service the basic security, health, and well-being of peoples around the world—including the people of the United States of America.

The chapter explains how the policy of Higher Realism deals with on the one hand the seeming contradiction between states and cultural communities' jealous protection of their sovereignty or autonomy and on the other hand the growing imperative of international cooperation generated by the proliferating material interdependence of peoples. The raw material for constructively transcending the apparent paralyzing dilemma is found in the cross-cutting relationships in the emergent polyarchy itself. The fact that many members of mutually antagonistic countries or communities are (or can be) cobeneficiaries or covictims of various developments or threats, and may well be (or can be induced to be) members of regional and global organizations for managing these developments or threats, is demonstrated in field after field: international air and oceanic transportation, global communications, banking and monetary affairs, trade, environmental protection, and arms control. The chapter indicates how this scaffolding of rudimentary international cooperation and accountability in these domains of unavoidable interdependence can be built upon. But I contend that the needed enhancement of such multilateral arrangements won't happen spontaneously, and certainly not to the degree necessary, without active and dedicated participation by the United States.

This observation raises the problem, which I address in Chapter 2 and I return to in Chapter 12, of selling such a new multilateralist thrust in U.S. foreign policy abroad and domestically given the hegemonic if not imperalist tenor of Washington's international assertiveness since the end of the Cold War. In other capitals, skeptics will be inclined to view it as a stratagem for assuring that foreign governments subordinate their policies to institutions the United States dominates. And at home, the likelihood of a neoisolationist backlash recent U.S. foreign policy failures, along with trepidation about taking on new international commitments in a world that has come to resent the United States so much, could frustrate efforts by an internationalist administration to obtain popular and congressional approval. Accordingly, there is a need to think through, carefully formulate, and credibly articulate how the security and well-being of the people of the United States require the servicing of a range of world interests that are also in the national interest. This is the challenge taken up by the rest of the book.

Chapters 3 through 10 focus on the world interests in the new foreign policy of Higher Realism: the healthy survival of the human species, a reduced reliance on force, the alleviation of extreme poverty and disease, a well-functioning global economy, the preservation of the planet's essential ecologies, the promotion of democracy and human rights, a culturally and religiously diverse world, and mutual accountability across borders. Each of these world interests is discussed in detail, including why it should be regarded as both a world interest and a high-priority national interest. The analysis in each chapter also traces out the broad policy and programmatic implications and offers preliminary assessments of the feasibility and desirability of alternative implementing strategies. The choice from among the alternative implementing strategies and their subsequent management is primarily the province of the country's public officials. But the evaluation of the contending alternatives should be informed by the basic philosophical approach of Higher Realism—namely, the melding of national and world interests—that is applied in each of these chapters to the relevant choices.

Chapter 11 indicates how the policy process—particularly in the interagency arena—can be adapted to carry out the proposed foreign policy, especially when it comes to establishing priorities and managing trade-offs among the basic interests and their implementing policies.

Chapter 12 returns to the problem of generating and sustaining popular support for the overall policy of Higher Realism and its emphasis on the connections between world interests, national interests, and the security and well-being of individual U.S. citizens and their families. Polls indicate that when citizens are shown these connections by committed policy elites, they will support the necessary international involvements even if the policies require drawing on the country's material and human resources. This has happened in the past, and if we are clearheaded about what the world and the country need today, it can happen now.

CHAPTER ONE

The Emergent Global System

T he security and well-being of the people of the United States can be seriously jeopardized if there is a mismatch between the ideas of those responsible for U.S. foreign policy about how the world works and the actual structure and behavior of the global system. Yet such a mismatch has, by and large, prevailed since the end of the Cold War.

To be consistent with the emerging realities, the formulation and the conduct of U.S. foreign policy must be freed of a number of fantasies and fallacies that have distorted views on the part of high officials and influential analysts about the distribution of power in the system and its appropriate uses.

First is what can be called the Double-O Delusion of omnipotence and omniscience: the belief that because of its great military strength and economic wealth, the United States has the power to prevail over any adversary or combination of adversaries that might temporarily attempt to prevent it from exercising its will and, further, that the success of the United States in achieving such military and economic primacy comes from being wiser than the others about the best way to organize human societies—nations, as well as the world community. Next is the Polarity Fallacy: deducing that the world is *uni*polar from the assumption that during the Cold War, the world was *bi*polar (except for the nonaligned countries) and from the fact that by the 1990s, the Soviet Union had opted out of its global rivalry with the United States.

The Double-O Delusion and the Polarity Fallacy were fused and reflected in both the assertive globalization pursued by the Clinton administration and the Bush administration's neoconservative agenda that gave us Operation Iraqi Freedom. Although most countries have adjusted their policies to the reality that there is now only one superpower, they have not bought into the fantasies of a post–Cold War Pax Americana, nor have many been drawn into the gravitational field of the presumed unipolar system.

Lately, policymakers and analysts in the United States and around the world have revived the concept of multipolarity to describe the emergent structure of international relations. But as I will show in this chapter, neither unipolarity nor multipolarity exists in fact.

The emergent global system of diffuse power and crosscutting relationships is more aptly conceptualized as a polyarchy. Recognizing the emergent Polyarchy for what it is—complex, disorderly, and volatile, such that today's close friend may be tomorrow's enemy—is a prerequisite for effective efforts to rid twenty-first-century world politics of its dangerous dysfunctional tendencies. Accordingly, analysis of these emergent global realities is the starting point for the foreign policy of Higher Realism.

Pax Americana and the Double-O Delusion

The expectation of global peace ultimately materializing from U.S. promotion of market democracy around the world—the vision of neo-conservatives and neo-Wilsonians alike—draws on the model of nineteenth-century "Pax Britannica." Britain, with its technologically advanced and ubiquitous navy, aspired not only to rule the waves but also to foster a free-trading global economic system highly favorable to the industrially superior and raw material–importing country. The Pax Britannica vision held that what was good for England was good for the world, since free markets and global commerce, protected by the Royal Navy, would "lift all [economic] boats" as the Adam Smith/David Ricardo predictions of product specialization on the basis of comparative advantage were at last permitted to materialize. The British convinced themselves (falsely, as it turned out) that as long as Britain was willing to absorb the costs of protecting free international commerce, most of the other countries would hop on the free-trade bandwagon and accept British hegemony.

The post–Cold War champions of Pax Americana in both political parties in the United States also hold that the globalization of the system of market democracies requires the leadership of an omnipotent and omniscient hegemon willing to take on the economic and political burdens of fostering and maintaining the system. "If we have to use force," explained Secretary of State Madeleine Albright, "it is because we are America! We are the indispensable nation, and we see further into the future."[1] In the wake of 9/11, a new urgency and rationale—the war against terrorism—was added to the Pax Americana mission. As articulated by Vice President Dick Cheney, "America has friends and allies in this cause, but only we can lead it.... The United States and only the United States can see this effort through to victory. This responsibility did not come to us by chance. We are in a unique position because of our unique assets, because of the character of our people, the strength of our ideals, and the might of our military and the enormous economy that supports it."[2]

Looking beyond Iraq, although failure in Iraq could produce an isolationist backlash, foreign policy spokespersons in both parties have regarded continuing U.S. primacy, particularly in the military sphere, as the indispensable condition for sustaining such a Pax Americana. U.S. military capabilities, strategies, and deployments, averred the Bush administration's basic national security strategy paper, are used to "create a balance of power that favors human freedom."[3] The new "forward strategy of freedom" was justified by the proposition that "in every region of the world, the advance of freedom leads to peace."[4]

The forecast of global peace flowing from a Kantian world of market democracies protected and instructed by the U.S. hegemon is based on the assumption that the successor to Cold War bipolarity is *uni*polarity. But this, too, is an illusion.

The False Promise of Unipolarity

Seeing one of the two power centers of the Cold War bipolar system collapse, its sphere of control disintegrate, particularly in Eastern Europe, and its satraps around the world left without a big-brother military ally and economic patron, many analysts, policymakers, and pundits deduced that the successor system, as long as the power of the United States remained intact, was *unipolar.*[5] By the standard (material) measures of power, this should still be the case. With a defense budget greater than the combined military budgets of the next fifteen countries, the United States fields the strongest and most technologically sophisticated conventional forces in the world, with military deployments in over 100 countries and over 6,000 nuclear warheads in its strategic nuclear arsenal.[6] The gross national product (GNP) of the United States—running well over $13 trillion a year—is 20 percent of the world's combined GNP.[7] And although it spends about two-tenths percent of its GNP on official development assistance—one of the lowest percentages among the affluent countries—this still amounts to a larger absolute amount of foreign aid (running at about $27 billion a year) than is provided by any other country.[8]

But how much effective influence over others does this great differential in material power confer? True, the United States, the only remaining superpower, is the most influential single actor, and its cooperation or opposition can often determine the fate of policies and programs of others around the world. But being the only superpower is not the same as having effective power over most others in the system. Some forms of power—military, economic, ideational, or the power that comes from diplomatic/political skill—may have an impact on some actors more than others, affected in each case by a multitude of material, cultural, and historical factors. These various types of power are often neither fungible nor fully additive into a kind of Gross National Power that when posed against the power of another state will overcome its resistance, like a magnet pulling on a piece of metal.

In other words, *super* power does not simply translate into *polar* power, in the sense of the impact exerted by the United States and the Soviet Union during the Cold War. The bipolarity of the Cold War system inhered not just in the existence of two countries more powerful than any of the rest but also in the massive gravitational pull (geostrategic and ideological) each superpower had on others.[9] Each superpower's influence over the international behavior of its allies and clients was so great that it was indeed appropriate to regard the whole system, except for the determinedly nonaligned countries,[10] as in a condition of two-sided polarization.

Ironically, since the demise of its superpower rival (and largely because of its demise), the United States has been less able to influence other nations to accede to its will than it was during the Cold War, even when applying its putative hegemonic weight—either benignly, through providing economic, security, and prestige benefits to those who cooperate, or coercively, through imposing punitive economic or political sanctions or wielding military power. Except in certain specifically defined post-9/11 counterterrorism projects, few countries have been all that ready to coalesce under the U.S. banner—the "bandwagoning" response to a hegemon's exertions of power. Rather, as became dramatically and painfully evident in the U.S. failure to gain United Nations Security Council backing for Operation Iraqi Freedom, many influential actors in the international community, including countries the United States used to count as loyal allies, are resisting being pushed around or bought off when their interests, values, or grand strategies diverge from those of the hegemon. For the most part, however, the resistance has taken the form of "balking" (the dynamics of which will be elaborated later, along with the polyarchy concept) rather than efforts to form a balancing coalition against the United States.

The Mirage of Multipolarity

If not the hegemonic peace conceptualized by the unipolarists—a world in which the United States, the omnipotent regent, dispenses rewards and threatens sanctions to maintain order in and among its otherwise unruly wards—could we see a revival of the traditional system of great-power alignments, power balancing, and concerts?[11] Perhaps there can yet be a multipolar equilibrium among the great powers, analogous to the multipolar systems of the past, in which power balancing among a number of major states (possibly five but as many as a dozen) was the key to international stability or a breakdown of world order and peace.[12]

The emerging twenty-first-century geopolitical reality, however, looks quite different from traditional multipolarity. Only two contemporary "great powers" are potential sources of serious threats to international peace and security in the near future: China, if it resorts to military means to take over Taiwan or becomes too aggressive in prosecuting its claims in the South China and East China Seas, and possibly Russia, if, emboldened by its new energy-based muscularity and resenting the post–Cold War constriction of its sphere of influence, it attempts to reassert dominance over former Soviet-controlled areas.[13] In the more distant future, Japan, if it converts its hefty "self-defense" forces into an all-purpose military and particularly if it develops its own nuclear arsenal, could come into military confrontation with Russia or China in ways that threaten overall peace and security.[14] The European Union (EU), which may be considered a great power when further consolidated, could progressively intensify both its economic and its diplomatic rivalry with the United States. Yet such economic and political conflicts as do emerge between the EU and the United States are highly unlikely to escalate to the level of threats of force, let alone war, unless they are preceded by some fundamental discontinuities in domestic and world politics.

The sources of internationally destabilizing actions are more likely to be middle powers such as Saudi Arabia and Iran (each seeking regional hegemony, with or without nuclear weapons) or nuclear-armed India and Pakistan in a new war over Kashmir or Israel and its neighbors—

particularly if their conflicts interfere with the industrial states' access to important economic resources or geostrategic locations. The greatest worry in regard to North Korea may be an implosion of its governing regime resulting from an inability to satisfy the basic needs of its people; should that occur, both its international marketing of nuclear-weapons components and its temptation to raise diversionary tensions with South Korea or Japan are potential serious threats to international peace and security. Failed or failing states—such as Zimbabwe, Bangladesh, Afghanistan (if current stabilization efforts collapse), or even Kosovo after the departure of the security forces of the North Atlantic Treaty Organization (NATO)—could catalyze dangerous regional instabilities. Moreover, the entire system can be destabilized by wars initiated and conducted by nongovernmental actors: violent political movements, terrorist networks, and criminal syndicates.

In the system maturing before us, the precipitating events more than ever (except perhaps in medieval Europe) are also likely to come in a variety of forms besides the movement of military forces across borders—terrorism, subnational and transnational ethnic wars, failed domestic political systems, collapsing economies, contraband in weapons and drugs, and ecological disasters.[15] Rivalries or concerted action among the great powers might be important in exploiting or countering various of these threats to international peace and security, but more often than not, the sources of war and peace will lie elsewhere than in the great-power competition.

In short, in contrast to the great-power multipolar systems of the past, there are now a much larger number and a greater variety of actors, both states and nonstate actors, that can shake up the system. The major threats to system equilibrium are not primarily territorial expansion, a tipping of the balance of power through the addition or subtraction of allies, or dramatic augmentation of one or another of the great powers' military capabilities. Opposition to the policies of a great power will rarely result in power balancing through the formation or tightening of countervailing alliances. More likely, opposition will come as irritating, even defiant, acts of noncooperation—what I call balking—such as the refusal of France, Russia, and China to vote with the United States on important Iraq resolutions before the Security Council or the refusal of Turkey to allow its territory to be used as a base for the invasion of Iraq.

The Emergent Polyarchy

The structure of world politics that has evolved since the end of the Cold War still features the global hegemony of the United States (not unipolarity) but, increasingly, within a *polyarchic* field of actors—nation-states, terrorist networks, subnational groups, transnational religions, multinational enterprises, and global and regional institutions. These communities and organizations are often in intense competition for resources and for the support and loyalty of their constituents, many of whom are members of several competing entities at the same time. Hardly any countries or political movements are unidirectionally aligned in their major international relationships, either with one another or with the United States. The cross pressures to which countries are subject in the emergent polyarchic system also make for volatile alignments and antagonisms. Allies on one issue may be adversaries on another issue; today's closest partner may well be tomorrow's most determined rival and vice versa, depending on the matter at hand.

The fact that many NATO countries and members of the Gulf War coalition of 1991 were at odds with the United States over how to deal with Saddam Hussein in 2003 was less an anomaly than an expression of the emergent Polyarchy. Unlike the Cold War system (or its hypothetical multipolar or unipolar successors), which assumed a high degree of congruence between primary security communities, trading blocs, and ideological coalitions, today's world society features a good deal of incongruence—not as an aberration but as a systemic characteristic. Trading partners, such as Canada and the United States, may be adversaries on military and arms-control issues (e.g., national missile defense, the Comprehensive Test Ban Treaty, and the ban on land mines) and on how to deal with difficult countries within the hemisphere, such as Cuba or Venezuela. Cultural/ideological allies, such as Sweden and Finland, may be in serious dispute over navigational and fishing rights. Countries engaged in joint military technology projects (Russia and the former Soviet states in Central Asia, for example) may have major differences over fighting terrorism or combating contraband in drugs. Allies on many global environmental issues (say, India and Malaysia) are frequently at odds on questions of human rights or humanitarian intervention. Similar in their views on Israeli-Palestinian issues, Saudi Arabia and Syria strongly differ over how to deal with Iran. Even Britain and the United States, close allies in Iraq and Afghanistan, have been far apart on how to combat global warming and on the role of the International Criminal Court. Moreover, such cross pressures are often rooted in a stratum of complex relationships at the substate level, wherein some sectors in a country want to retain and institutionalize cooperative interaction with particular sectors in nations toward which other sectors are hostile; this is a characteristic feature of the U.S.-British-French-German relationships, of relationships among the EU countries themselves, and increasingly of the relationship between the Japanese and the Chinese.[16] Then, too, domestic political changes, empowering elites who want to alter the direction of their country's foreign policies—sometimes bringing about a divergence, sometimes a convergence with U.S. policies—further add to the uncertainties about which countries can be depended upon to be international partners over the long run.

Accordingly, it is becoming difficult for governments around the world to enter into and sustain reliable alliance commitments and collective security arrangements for dealing with potential threats from adversaries. Individual nations must prepare to fend for themselves—or opportunistically seek allies of convenience for prosecuting the conflict at hand (as the United States did in Operation Iraqi Freedom). And in the process, they are loosening the constraints on unilateral action that are supposed to prevail in multilateral security communities.

Despite NATO's invocation of its founding treaty's Article V solidarity commitment in response to the September 11 terrorist attacks and despite official reaffirmations of the crucial role that alliances play in U.S. national security policy, Washington's defense planning has had to adapt to a world of weakening alliances and increasing non-alignment. Even before the problem became manifest in Afghanistan and Iraq, the 2001 Quadrennial Defense Review was calling for "the capability to send well-armed and logistically supported forces to critical points around the globe, even ... to locations where the support infrastructure is lacking or has collapsed" (code words for "we may not have supportive allies in the locale of a crucial military operation, but we need to be able to get there and fight nonetheless").[17] Anticipating future conflicts in which there may be no allies along the route to the zone of conflict who are willing to provide ports and large airfields, the Department of Defense has been putting a premium on high-speed sealift and ultraheavy airlift, plus platforms for midcourse refueling.

Such "alliance-insensitive" military strategies and capabilities are facilitated by innovations in military technology brought on by the so-called Revolution in Military Affairs. Advances in information technology, for example, that permit a high degree of interoperability among the national components of a multilateral coalition also allow those components to disengage from a coalition military operation without paralyzing the multinational system or seriously interfering with the effectiveness of those who want to proceed.

In short, the U.S. military is being transformed into an institution that can operate globally with very few allies or even without allies when necessary. As this transformation matures, there will be less need of allied concurrence before undertaking major military moves. And ostensible allies, coming to understand that they are little valued and are even considered an encumbrance, are more and more motivated to develop their own capabilities to go it alone in situations where the United States does not consider its interests to be sufficiently at risk. The trend in military planning thus not only reflects but also reinforces the tendencies in Polyarchy that work against concerted multilateral action in the peace and security field.

The world might seem to be reverting to the traditional self-help system of determinedly sovereign nation-states. But the "anarchy" of the traditional system was, by comparison, quite stable. National leaders could by and large control what went on within their jurisdictions and could quite reliably commit their countries to alliances in order to counter the power of their aggressive adversaries. In the polyarchic world, there are many more "loose cannons" (literally and figuratively) capable on their own of generating havoc in the system, destabilizing governments as well as international peace and security arrangements. Osama bin Laden is one such actor, of course, but so, too, are transnational entrepreneurs, pirates of weapons and high-tech knowledge, and even respectable multinational corporations with a vested interest in who runs the government in countries where they have subsidiaries.

Alternative U.S. Responses to Polyarchy

An adaptive U.S. response to the emergent Polyarchy would entail, first of all, the recognition that its emergence is systemic, not some temporary aberration. The next step would be to translate this understanding into a foreign policy, consistent with U.S. resources and values, that the public can be expected to support. There are four plausible alternative foreign policies. The first I call Pax Americana with Teeth, meaning a continuation of the neoconservative/neo-Wilsonian policy of interventions—multilateral if feasible, unilateral if necessary, peaceful if possible, but with the augmented "hard power" required to implement the policy—in order to stabilize and democratize violence-prone societies around the world. The second policy is Neo-isolationism, avoiding entangling multilateral commitments, resisting globalization trends that limit U.S. self-sufficiency, washing America's hands of the world's great unwashed, and making the country once again a "city on a hill" that knows what it wants for itself but does not try to actively convert others to the American way. The third possible foreign policy is Conventional Realism, a more patient response to the polyarchic complexities; this approach is marked by avoiding intrusive involvement in areas of instability and chaos that do not impact substantially on U.S. vital interests and relying mostly on the sovereignty-respecting diplomacy of state-to-state bargaining rather than political and military intervention to resolve disputes. And finally, there is Higher Realism, my recommended policy—to be elaborated in the subsequent chapters—for melding vital U.S. interests with essential global security and humanitarian interests while embracing the political, economic, and cultural *diversity* of world society and, at the same time, championing global norms, rules, and processes of mutual international accountability (binding on the United States as well as others) for managing the deepening interdependence of peoples.

Pax Americana with Teeth

Appealing to those of hawkish—and noble—disposition, this ambitious policy (although abjuring the Pax Americana label) purports to be the nation's historically destined response to the contemporary threats to homeland security and to world order: rogue states that flout their international obligations, transnational terrorists and states that sponsor or harbor them, and failed or failing states. The strategy assumes that it may not be enough to attempt to militarily deter such governments or movements from hostile acts against the world or to dissuade them with carrot-and-stick diplomacy from grossly mistreating or neglecting their own people. It may require going to war to effect a change in regime, as in the deposition of the Taliban in Afghanistan and Saddam Hussein in Iraq, or "humanitarian intervention" with major military force, as in Bosnia and Kosovo.

The ascendancy of this view in the foreign policy community constitutes a double irony. The first irony is that many of the foreign policy liberals who became prominent antiwar doves during the Vietnam War and its aftermath were reincarnated, as it were, as neo-Wilsonian interventionists during the Clinton-Gore years. Quite a number of them carried the Wilsonian renaissance forward into John F. Kerry's 2004 presidential campaign and into the campaigns of the leading contenders for the Democratic Party's nomination in 2008—reflecting the central argument of *The Responsibility to Protect* report prepared by the Canadian-sponsored International Commission on Intervention and State Sovereignty: "Where a population is suffering serious harm, as a result of internal war, insurgency or state failure, and the state in question is unwilling or unable to halt or avert it, the principle of nonintervention yields to the responsibility to protect."[18] The second irony is that the Pax Americana imperatives were adopted after 9/11 by a president whose election campaign had vilified the Clinton-Gore administration for its globalist do-goodism and allegedly naive policy of nation-building in the failed states. The United States, under the guidance of George W. Bush's neoconservative gurus, was now in the business of *civilization*-building around the world on the pillars of political and economic freedom and democracy.[19]

The virtue of the Pax Americana policy is that it shows the United States as standing for purposes beyond the perpetuation of its own primacy. The problems, however, are manifold: most important, it violates the fundamental precept of foreign policy prudence by establishing global commitments that cannot be sustained without a degree of investment of U.S. material resources, and potentially of military manpower, that is politically unsustainable at home. As the achievements fall far short of the promises, there are backlashes around the world to U.S. professions of global responsibility and leadership; allegations of double standards and hypocrisy as the resource crunch compels a highly selective policy that favors some countries over others; and encouragement for adversaries of the United States, such as Hugo Chavez of Venezuela, to increase the decibel level of their vilifications of Washington. Moreover, Washington's former Cold War allies, no longer needing to depend on the United States for their own security, are increasingly resentful of the presumption that being the "indispensable superpower" gives the United States the prerogative to call the shots in designing and managing the new world order, particularly when Washington, feeling too constrained by the multilateral institutions and treaties it previously championed, insists on the privileges of unilateral action.[20]

Neo-isolationism

In the context of growing national anguish over the blood and treasure costs of a hubristic military operation to render a part of the world safe for freedom, today's isolationists are able to make their arguments to an attentive audience. The upsurge in anti-Americanism around the world, inflamed by the U.S. occupation of Iraq (but antedating it), has stimulated the Neo-isolationists on both the Left and the Right to press their case with renewed vigor, in essence declaring, "The foreigners don't want us, so let's come home."[21] The intellectual expression of the isolationist impulse—the flip side of the impulse to transform the world in America's own image (the former a reaction to the latter's frustration)—has appeared in a spate of post-9/11 books and articles inveighing against the alleged disposition by those now running U.S. foreign policy to establish a global imperium.[22]

The current isolationism, however, is more than a temporary backlash against ascendant neoconservative/neo-Wilsonian views. Its has deep roots in the nationalist and populist soil of the country, now being cultivated and watered, of course, by antiglobalization politicians who are catering to sectors of the population that fear economic displacement as U.S. firms relocate abroad to take advantage of lower factor costs. Why, the antiglobalists ask, should any sacrifices be borne to make the world safe for American investments when these are the investments of the very multinational firms that are transferring jobs and productive facilities to other countries? The new isolationism also has cultural sources and expressions, some quite openly xenophobic, of hostility toward the one-world, global-market, open-borders approach, an approach that is perceived to be diluting the American Way of Life and undermining the country's role as a "city on a hill" to be envied and eventually emulated by others.[23]

The isolationist response to Polyarchy, like the Pax Americana response, is one of *non*accommodation to the chaos "out there." But rather than trying to police and reform the outside world, the isolationists contend that the United States should do a better job of insulating itself from the cultural and physical viruses. Globalists praise the new electronic technologies for finally allowing the dream of an integrated world market to be realized; Neo-isolationists, by contrast, argue these technologies should be applied to securing and strengthening borders and barriers against the free ingress of goods and people—not simply as part of the war on terrorism but also to keep out the carriers of societal dissipation and corruption.

The technological and economic forces of international interdependence and global integration have matured too far, however, and they benefit too many sectors of American society for the isolationist response to Polyarchy to appeal to more than a minority of the citizenry, let alone to become the official U.S. worldview. Yet because of their concentration in particular electoral districts and because of the intensity of some of their grievances, the Neo-isolationists, by virtue of the seniority of their representatives in the House and the Senate, can often seriously constrain and inhibit policies they regard as too internationalist.

Conventional Realism

From the standpoint of what can be called Conventional Realism,[24] the response to the volatility and uncertainties of the emergent Polyarchy should be a patient U.S. foreign policy for dealing with particular challenges as they arise—but selectively, giving clear priority to preventing an attack on the homeland and preserving access to foreign sources of oil.[25] The post–Cold War Realists tend to favor a statecraft of bargaining rather than hegemonic diktat, albeit backed up by unambiguous military superiority so as to discourage others from escalating disputes with the United States to the level of violence.[26] Recognizing that most disputes the United States has or is likely to have with other countries do not and need not jeopardize the irreducible U.S. national interest (the physical security of the citizenry, the country's economic well-being, and its basic constitutional system),[27] Realists believe that U.S. foreign policy should be able to adhere to Hans Morgenthau's fourth fundamental rule of diplomacy: "Nations must be willing to compromise on all issues that are not vital to them."[28] And in the bargaining over secondary and tertiary interests, you win some and lose some.

The Conventional Realist's counsel to this generation of U.S. leaders and the public at large is that the United States, although the only remaining superpower, should use its power prudentially and not expend it in futile attempts to run the whole system. Nor should the United States intervene in the domestic affairs of other countries unless intervention is required to secure the fundamental U.S. national interest. In extreme cases (such as the need to smash terrorists with a global reach) or in cases of horrendous human rights violations (such as genocide), that requirement might well warrant a regime-change operation. But any such overriding of the state-sovereignty norm should have the widest possible international writ of approval, should be situation-specific, and should eschew the imperial conceit of prescribing the best way of life for all people.

Some of the most prominent scholars of this disposition were quite vocal in opposing the neoconservative thrust of foreign policy under George W. Bush that resulted in Operation Iraqi Freedom.[29] Many of them banded together as the Coalition for a Realistic Foreign Policy, writing op-ed pieces and speaking against forcible regime-change policies even against tyrannical states.[30] The Realists have been divided, however, about resorting to military action to hobble Iran's or North Korea's nuclear weapon capabilities, arguing over whether such operations would be unrealistic and dangerously provocative and whether such "rogue states" can be deterred from actually using weapons of mass destruction (WMD) should they opt to deploy them.

The problem with the Conventional Realist response is that it is long on what the United States should *not* attempt to do yet short on what can and should be done to counteract the chaos and often violent eruptions in the emerging Polyarchy. It views the world as essentially stymied when it comes to preventing the spread of WMD, effectively counteracting global warming, and alleviating the starvation and disease of billions of people—recognizing this paralysis as a symptom of the still largely anarchic international system. But traditional Realism has no vision of system transformation, let alone global governance, for ameliorating the looming dangers.[31]

Higher Realism

The fourth of the alternative responses is Higher Realism. It shares with Conventional Realism the insistence that the United States, in acting to influence conditions abroad, must give priority to the vital national interests of the country—securing the homeland against physical attack, sustaining the economic well-being of the American people, and preserving their basic liberties. And it, too, holds that the grand strategy for serving these national interests must be consistent with both U.S. resources and the international distribution of power, especially (though not exclusively) coercive power. Like Conventional Realism, Higher Realism requires that particular policies be chosen prudently, on the basis of a clearheaded evaluation that a set of conditions is having or is likely to have a significant impact on U.S. interests, that the policies can indeed affect these conditions in desirable ways, that the expected benefits from the prospective course of action are worth its expected costs, and that the American people and their representatives in Congress can be convinced to provide the necessary human and material resources. But Higher Realism does not share Conventional Realism's tendency to discount the nonmaterial components of power and the importance of international institutions and norms.

A Higher Realist foreign policy would be based on the recognition of how inextricably bound up U.S. national interests have become with *world* interests—with the security and well-being of people everywhere. But it would reject the Pax Americana hubris that what is good for the United States is, ipso facto, good for the world.

Higher Realism regards the enhancement of international accountability norms and institutions—a rule-based global system—as necessary for the country's long-term security and well-being, despite the fact that those norms and institutions may sometimes constrain the United States from acting with complete flexibility.[32] Higher Realism understands how

41

U.S. military superiority and economic primacy, and the will to invoke them coercively at times, remain essential components of U.S. power for securing the country's national interests. Yet it also appreciates the importance of subjecting any coercive use of U.S. material power to widely accepted standards of legitimacy so as not to undermine the "soft" components of power that are required to induce others to cooperate in building the rule-based global system.

Higher Realism insists that the security and well-being of the people of the United States, not simply moral altruism, require a determined effort to reduce the vast amount of poverty and disease in the world. And it asserts that the United States must again take a leading role (which it has abjured since 2000) in forging global cooperation to preserve the planet's temperate climate and to husband its scarce resources and natural ecologies.

Higher Realism supports the evolution of political systems that are based on the informed consent of the governed and respectful of human rights. But it opposes attempts to universalize the American way of life as *the* way of organizing society and to project it onto the world's culturally diverse nations. Rather, both as an end itself, consistent with the continuing *e pluribus unum* experiment that is the essence of the country, and because otherwise U.S. foreign policy will generate increasing hostility, the United States should be a champion, not an adversary, of a culturally and religiously diverse world. Under these premises, the United States would be generally supportive of efforts by distinct cultural communities across the globe to practice their own ways of life and to devise their own political and economic systems, and it would refrain from intervening to compel them to emulate the U.S. or other "Western" models. This approach should not, however, preclude interventions, legitimized by a broad international consensus, to counter genocide and other crimes against humanity as defined in the statute of the new International Criminal Court. Nor should such forbearance prevent the United States from engaging in internationally authorized peacekeeping or conflict-control operations where they are required to prevent an eruption of violence.

The difficulty with the foreign policy of Higher Realism is not its lack of correspondence with the emergent Polyarchy or with its capacity to serve the many U.S. interests that require the cooperation of other nations. The difficulty lies, rather, in how hard it may be to generate sufficient domestic public and even elite support for long-term international community-building policies that, in the absence of a dramatic threat to the security and well-being of the American people, are not obviously required for servicing the immediate and tangible interests of the country.[33] In the following chapters, I attempt to systematically make the case for Higher Realism to members of the policy community and the attentive public, trusting that among those I hope to persuade, there will be organizational, rhetorical, and media skills for helping to generate the required popular support.

Meanwhile, How Is the World Responding?

In the emergent Polyarchy, one is less likely to encounter the typical responses to an overbearing hegemon (in this era, the United States) than in previous international systems. To be sure, some countries and political movements have been following the U.S. lead—the traditional bandwagoning dynamic—fearful of alienating the hegemon and seeking the positive benefits of loyal support. But as Prime Minister Tony Blair in England and Prime Minister José Maria Aznar in Spain each discovered, bandwagoning will often prove to be highly unpopular with nationalistic constituents. Others, such as governments catalyzed by Islamicist resentments, may try to balance the power of the United States—either benignly, through anti-U.S. coalitions in international forums and discriminatory commercial blocs, or dangerously, through conspiring to harass and play havoc with Americans and their assets around the world.

Most governments, however, are attempting to avoid the pitfalls of either bandwagoning or balancing. Rather, when caving in to the imperious hegemon can be politically embarrassing but striking a posture of frontal defiance can be too risky, the favored strategy of weaker states more and more often is balking—my term for determined nonalignment along with clever self-interested bargaining.[34]

Here are some varieties of the balking strategy:

- Refusing to cooperate with a particular U.S. policy not out of any profound philosophical or geostrategic disagreement but simply to induce the United States to be more forthcoming on issues deemed more vital to the balking state (Mexico's often-irritating vocal opposition to U.S. policies on global security issues in order to get the United States to be more responsive to Mexico's positions on cross-border migration appears to be of this sort);
- Refusing to agree to a specific request because to do so would be risky domestically, not out of any motive to balance or delegitimize U.S. power (e.g., Turkey's refusal to allow U.S. forces to cross through its territory in Operation Iraqi Freedom);
- Finding ways to indicate that one is not completely in the pocket of the United States (such as the Polish government's decision to terminate its deployment of troops in Iraq largely out of Warsaw's pique at not being taken seriously enough by Washington);
- Insisting on subjecting U.S. démarches to authorization by multilateral forums in which U.S. influence will be diluted (e.g., the French and German strategies for reigning in U.S. policies toward Iraq);
- Pursuing one's own grand strategy of diversifying one's dependency relationships and thus enhancing one's bargaining position overall (as with much of what is going on in Central Asia today on the part of Uzbekistan and others in reaction to U.S. and Russian efforts to turn them into more permanent military allies);
- Not cooperating fully with U.S. demands, even in the security field, because of commercial/economic motives, not necessarily out of a calculated strategy to be difficult (e.g., Russian, Chinese, and even Israeli international sales of nuclear power items that could be dual purpose and general arms sales to governments against U.S. wishes);

- Engaging in "linkage" diplomacy against the United States (such as China's favoring Airbus over Boeing in retaliation for anti-Chinese positions taken by the United States in the Human Rights Commission); and
- Disagreeing publicly with the wisdom of U.S. policy (such as South Korea's statements on how to deal with Pyongyang or Canada's disagreements with the United States on various arms policies and on relations with Cuba) by governments that know they will not be coercively sanctioned by the United States even though Washington is irritated.

Such balking strategies, given the crosscutting relationships in the emergent Polyarchy, are becoming a standard feature of international diplomacy. They were by no means absent from Cold War diplomacy (notably, "nonaligned" countries such as India and Indonesia developed them into a high art form). But the disappearance of the Cold War imperatives championed by the United States for containing the rival superpower has created a more permissive environment for balking and (except in relation to counterterrorism and counterproliferation imperatives) has removed Washington's "moral" justification for demanding conformity from others. Indeed, the current widespread balking at U.S. demands is *systemically* determined, being a function of the emerging Polyarchy, and it can be expected to grow in the decades ahead.

But meanwhile, unless these self-interest-only norms of Polyarchy are somehow transcended, global public goods essential to the security and well-being of people around the world will be neglected. To overcome the structural and behavioral obstacles to the collaboration required to provide these public goods, the major international actors—especially the U.S. government and powerful entities in the private sector—will have to give high priority to the world interests consistent with the Higher Realist agenda elaborated in the following chapters.

CHAPTER TWO

Realism

Conventional and Higher

I n common usage, *realism* means simply to view (or deal with) the world as it is—without illusions. Anyone formulating or conducting U.S. foreign policy would want to be, in that sense, a realist. Yet there is plenty of disagreement among analysts and practitioners over what the world is really like and therefore over what policies are realistic or unrealistic.

Growing out of such debates, an influential school of thought has developed whose adherents claim to be the *real* realists. And though its self-assessment is challenged by some scholars of world politics and international relations specialists, the particular worldview it has championed has come to be widely identified within the profession as the realist paradigm. To distinguish this worldview from the ordinary claim most of us make of being realists, I always capitalize its moniker as Realism and call its adherents Realists.

As I intend to make clear, *Higher* Realism endorses many, but not all, of the tenets of what has come to be called Realism. Higher Realism adds tenets of its own and substantially modifies the thrust of Conventional Realism, for the standard Realist paradigm fails to adequately comprehend the emergent Polyarchy—its threats and opportunities. And therefore, a U.S. foreign policy based on Conventional Realist premises, however welcome a reaction to the Pax Americana excesses following 9/11, will not be an effective servant of U.S. and world interests in the years ahead.

Conventional Realism

Realism has a number of branches with their own special names and analytical concepts: Classical Realism, Neorealism, Structural Realism, Offensive Realism, and others.[1] Despite the variations, however, they all embrace the essential assumptions of the standing Realist paradigm, which I call Conventional Realism—namely, that the world's political system is (and is destined to stay) fundamentally anarchic, in that it lacks a central authority with the power to make and enforce binding rules on the world's peoples. Such rule-making and rule-enforcing authority and power is lodged primarily in the governments of territorially bounded countries (or nation-states) and, periodically in certain regions, in empires. Consequently, each country, in order to maintain its realm and its people and to secure its territorial integrity, sovereign independence, and way of life, must depend on its own power (perhaps augmented by help from allies) relative to other countries that might try to impose their will on it. Acquiring and husbanding such power to prevent being controlled or pushed around by others is, therefore, the most vital imperative.

Most Conventional Realists regard a country's military capabilities and economic assets that can be used coercively as *the* trump cards in the competitive balance-of-power game. Thus, we have the much-repeated aphorism that force is the *ultima ratio* of international politics and the frequently quoted rendition by Thucydides of the Athenian generals' statement to the Melians that "the strong do what they can and the weak suffer what they must." The need to have plenty of "hard power" in order to conduct effective statecraft in the anarchic system is accordingly transformed into an end in itself, one of the country's irreducible national interests.

Conventional Realism also, and not surprisingly, discounts the role of international law and institutions in world society, regarding these as little more than epiphenomenal reflections of the international distribution of hard power. Similarly, with regard to demands for global justice, Realists are inclined to project into the international arena the contention of Thrasymachus in Plato's *Republic* that prevailing norms of justice are simply "what is to the interest of the stronger party."

Conventional Realism, however—despite its claim to be driven by hard interests and not ideology—does endorse (at least implicitly) the traditional norm of international relations that countries should not intervene in each other's domestic affairs. This state-sovereignty norm, an enduring legacy of the Peace of Westphalia (1648) ending the wars of religion that had been devastating central Europe, holds that how national governments run their own societies and treat the people within their own jurisdictions should not be the business of other governments, unless intervention is required by international balance-of-power or international security considerations. The norm has been qualified since World War II to permit intervention in order to prevent acts of genocide, and today's Conventional Realists are not adverse to violating state sovereignty for that purpose when such interventions can succeed. But they will usually object to a further eroding of the state-sovereignty norm for lesser "humanitarian" purposes, and they are philosophically opposed to efforts to legitimize and institutionalize a *global* responsibility to protect populations whose security, health, economic well-being, or basic civil and political rights are not being adequately ensured.

Translated into guidance for U.S. foreign policy, Conventional Realism applies a stern prudential test to all international actions and commitments by the U.S. government, asking: How do they contribute to the irreducible national interests—physical security, economic well-being, and basic way of life—of the United States? How do they maintain these conditions, in the words of the Constitution, for "*our*selves and

49

our posterity"? Actions or programs for affecting conditions outside the country must be based on informed judgments by policymakers that a particular set of conditions is having, or will have, a significant impact on U.S. interests; that the U.S. policies can significantly affect these conditions; and that the expected benefits to the United States from the actions or programs will be worth the expected costs.

The opposition to the Vietnam War by prominent American Realists, including diplomat George Kennan and international relations theorist Hans Morgenthau, proceeded from their strategic assessment that a Communist takeover of South Vietnam, although a negative development, would not significantly change the global balance of power in ways threatening to U.S. vital interests; further, the lives and material resources being sacrificed to prevent Ho Chi Minh's victory were not worth it. Four decades later, Conventional Realists in the Coalition for a Realistic Foreign Policy opposed Operation Iraqi Freedom—objecting especially to the Bush administration's insistence that, whether or not Iraq had an active nuclear weapons program, the United States had a vital interest in forcibly deposing Saddam Hussein and installing a democratic regime in Baghdad, for this would stimulate democratization throughout the Middle East and therefore pacification of the region. The Realists, most of whom had supported the 1991 Gulf War to repel Iraq's military occupation of Kuwait, now rejected the proposition that getting rid of Saddam's brutal dictatorship justified a U.S. military occupation of Iraq, even if this did lead to the spread of democracy in the Middle East—which, in the eyes of the Realists, would not really overcome the deeper sources of violent conflict in the region.

Higher Realism

Higher Realism agrees with much of the Conventional Realist critique of both the "indispensable superpower" chest-thumping of the Clinton administration and the imperious interventionism of the Bush administration since 9/11. The "double-O" conceit of omnipotence and omniscience—the illusion (and rhetorical claims) of being not only powerful enough but also wise enough to determine under what kind of political and economic regimes people should live around the world—has undermined Washington's real international power. Neither assertive neo-Wilsonianism nor neoconservatism provided a sound basis for conducting U.S. foreign policy in their claim that a country's internal political economy—in particular whether or not it was a democracy and had a market economy—was the principal criterion for treating it as friend or foe. Moreover, as the U.S. actions during both the Clinton years and the Bush years often blatantly contradicted this ideological posturing (for example, Clinton's reneging on his campaign promise to link normal trade with China to its progress on human rights and George W. Bush's signing up dictators and human rights abusers as antiterrorist allies), the credibility of U.S. commitments would be severely compromised, and its diplomacy could be accused of double standards and hypocrisy.

Higher Realism shares with Conventional Realism the understanding that in this still largely anarchic (though increasingly polyarchic) world, U.S. military and economic strength and the will to invoke them coercively at times remain essential components of U.S. power for securing the country's national interests. But Higher Realism, unlike Conventional Realism, emphasizes the importance of subjecting coercive applications of U.S. material power to widely accepted standards of legitimacy to avoid undermining the "soft" components of power required to induce others to cooperate in building a rule-based global system.

Higher Realism also shares with Conventional Realism the view that the first imperative of U.S foreign policy is to serve the irreducible national interests of the United States: the security of the homeland against catastrophic attacks; the economic well-being of the whole society; and the perpetuation of the American Way of Life. Foreign policy officials must give these basic *national* interests priority over both *sub*national local or special interests and *trans*national religious, cultural, or economic interests.

Priority is one thing; exclusive emphasis is another. Higher Realism is not satisfied with Conventional Realism's narrow-lens focus on the irreducible national interests. Rather, Higher Realism is intensely occupied with how inextricably bound up U.S. national interests have become with *world* interests—with the security and well-being of people everywhere. It rejects the conceit that what is good for the United States is, ipso facto, good for the world. But it operates from the understanding that what is good for the world as a whole is almost always good for the United States and that the United States, in its own interest and also morally because the country is so well endowed, should regard it as a national obligation to service the world interests and to contribute substantially to the provision of global public goods.

The Concept of World Interests

World interests are those conditions, natural or created by humans, that are in the interest of the entire human population. I use the term *interest* as Conventional Realists do, to denote what significantly affects the survival, well-being, and functioning of the entity of reference—the nation-state in Conventional Realism, the nation *and* world society in Higher Realism. Realist assessments, Conventional or Higher, of whether some condition is, indeed, in the interest of the country or world are supposed to be objective—that is, subject to empirical verification and reasoned judgment.

The focus on interests, so defined, does not exclude values—meaning strongly held and often philosophically embraced preferences. Some of the interests may be more highly valued than others by different segments of the population and leadership, and there may be considerable debate, therefore, over which interests should be accorded priority as well as a greater effort to secure them. Moreover, insofar as Realist concepts of national or world interests include the well-being of the society and since well-being obviously is a psychological dimension, the overall national or world interest must, in this respect, be partly subjective. The way this subjective (well-being) element can be handled objectively is to take explicit account of how the varying preferences—ranging from levels of prosperity to ethnic self-determination—will affect the value of and thus the priority to be accorded to the different interests and the policies designed to serve them. Just as such values issues must be dealt with in defining the national interests and the selection of policies to serve them, so they must be dealt with when defining and serving world interests. I will give special attention to the appropriate processes and institutions for doing this at the international level in chapter 10.

How, then, do we know or on what basis can we claim that some condition is in the interest of the world, the entire human population? First would be whatever is essential to the very survival of the human species—the continuation of human life, which could be threatened by a natural event such as an asteroid crashing into Earth, by a global "nuclear winter" resulting from a full-scale nuclear war in which clouds from the fallout blocked the Sun's rays from reaching the surface of the planet; or by an extreme acceleration of global warming. Although these catastrophic events are very unlikely, feasible measures to prevent them or reduce their probability are surely in the world interest (and are global public goods), even though the amount of resources to be devoted to such measures and the timing of their adoption would be highly controversial within countries and among countries.

The avoidance of other globally harmful but noncatastrophic conditions or events and the positive exploitation of conditions or situations to better the lives of people around the globe are also presumptively in the world interest, particularly if such efforts help to transform world society into a community. Although the terms *world community* or *international community* are frequently used, global society as a whole still falls far short of being a community. It is a society with more and more interdependence and with some regional and functional community arrangements, but it is not really a comprehensive community. When members of a society morally embrace the fact of their interdependence and foster norms of mutual accountability and responsibility, the society becomes a community.

But even as a society and not yet a community, the world system as a whole requires certain things, certain conditions for its effective functioning and for the rudimentary well-being of most of its members. At best, the members' interdependence will generate a mutual commitment to promote one another's well-being; minimally, interdependence will compel arrangements designed to avoid threatening one another's vital national interests; and at worst, the interdependence can lead to bitter conflicts of interest and internecine warfare. To the extent that the United States recognizes and responds to the need to begin transforming world society into a genuine world community—and this is the implication of the Higher Realist paradigm—its foreign policy will prominently feature efforts to institutionalize transnational accountability and responsibility and to develop reliable means of providing for global public goods.

Global Public Goods

Global public goods are almost identical to world interests. A global public good, as defined by economists, benefits people everywhere in the world. When such a good is provided, no country can be prevented from enjoying its benefits; when not provided, everybody loses. Furthermore, no community's enjoyment of it exhausts its availability for others.[2] Thus, one quintessential global public good would be the interception and destruction of a huge asteroid headed for planet Earth. Another would be the prevention or avoidance of dangerous levels of global warming.

Other examples are the care of natural resources and ecologies essential to the community's well-being, the provision and maintenance of infrastructures for worldwide communication and transportation, a workable international economic system for exchanging goods and services, at least a rudimentary system for peacefully resolving disputes among members, and the ability to protect the community arrangements and structures against terrorism and other destructive attacks.

All global public goods are also world interests. But not all world interests necessarily satisfy the economists' criteria for global public goods. Most countries, for example, regard the further proliferation of nuclear weapons as a world interest that is also in their national interest. But some countries, such as India, have refused to join the nuclear nonproliferation regime; for them, it is intolerable that only five countries (including China but not India or others in the group) are deemed responsible enough to possess nuclear weapons.

One overarching world interest, which is also a global public good, is transnational accountability—that is, mutual accountability across established borders among those who significantly affect one another's lives. The degree and type of accountability that it will be feasible to institute in various fields and among various sets of interacting players is the subject of one of the later chapters. The point here is that Higher Realism has as its normative core—for both pragmatic and moral reasons—the principle that *those who can or do crucially affect the security and well-being of others, especially by inflicting harm on them, are answerable to those they immediately and directly affect and to the larger society whose well-being, norms, and behavior are implicated.*

Serving world interests and providing such global public goods are not merely good works occasionally added on to the main imperatives of U.S. foreign policy for purposes of garnering international support for what Washington wants to do in its own self-interest. Rather, in the Higher Realism paradigm, they are part and parcel of the definition of the national interest itself.

Ensuring the Healthy Survival
of the Human Species

The healthy survival of the human species cannot be taken for granted, for humankind's greatest asset—its superior brain-power—paradoxically has put our own species at risk. That marvelous intellect has figured out how to take apart and recombine aspects of the natural world so as to dramatically alter the conditions of our existence. Some of our highly organized national communities, in order to protect themselves from attack and intrusion, have developed enough instruments of mass destruction to make the planet uninhabit-able: indeed, if only a fraction of these weapons were detonated, the continued healthy survival of the human species would be in jeopardy. And to warm ourselves when we feel too cold, to cool ourselves when we feel too hot, and to be able to move ourselves and things from place to place rapidly and efficiently, we have inadvertently been distorting the precious heat balance on Earth that has allowed human life to evolve. Consequently, the healthy survival of the human species has become the prime world interest—that is, an objective that must be actively secured and sustained. This interest dwarfs all other world, national, and special interests, being the essential condition for their realization.

Translating the healthy survival interest into high-priority policies is difficult and controversial because the two most serious threats—a full-scale nuclear war between major powers and dangerous levels of excessive global warming—appear to be either very unlikely to occur, in the first case, or remote in time, in the second. Moreover, because the threats are only hypothetical and the scientific predictions about their impacts are at best informed estimates based on models containing many unproven assumptions, policies offered to counter the threats must also involve considerable guesswork as to their effectiveness. Particularly when such policies carry a high price tag, the uncertainties tend to encourage a postponement of decisive action. Meanwhile, the lack of adequate attention to the threats and their potential effects may be adding to both the probability of their occurrence and the eventual costs of dealing with their consequences.

Preventing Nuclear Holocaust

The threat of all-out war between the two nuclear superpowers that preoccupied policymakers and publics during the Cold War has abated. Yet the United States and Russia each maintain some 6,000 deliverable strategic nuclear weapons in their active arsenals, and these weapons still carry sufficient explosive megatonnage to incinerate both countries and spread terrible illness and death far beyond their borders. Even if Moscow and Washington faithfully adhere to their latest strategic arms–reduction agreements and pare down their respective strategic deployments to about 2,000 intercontinental-range nuclear weapons (averaging 1 megaton), each side would retain a strategic force with the explosive power of more than 100,000 Hiroshima bombs.

If most of these remaining U.S. and Russian nuclear weapons were ever to be detonated in an exchange of strategic blows, the immediate blast effects alone would be equivalent to an explosion of 4 billion tons of TNT, and they would then be massively compounded by enormous firestorms. Some physicists and meteorologists have predicted that a holocaust of this magnitude would bring on a "nuclear winter": the nuclear explosions, particularly groundbursts, would lift tremendous amounts of particulate matter into the atmosphere; cloudbursts would generate fine dust; and the fires ignited by airbursts over cities and military installations would produce vast amounts of smoke—all of this blocking the sun's rays and causing surface temperatures to drop catastrophically, for months or even years. Crops and farm animals would freeze. And at least in the Northern Hemisphere, most human survivors would starve.[1]

Nuclear wars between some of the other major powers would pose less of a threat to the healthy survival of humankind as a whole, assuming such wars would not catalyze a larger world war. But at least one study of the nuclear winter effect estimated that even in a war involving the explosion of less than 1 percent of the world's arsenals and only low-yield airbursts over cities, the thousands of fires that would be ignited would generate an epoch of cold almost as severe as would be caused by an all-out U.S.-Russian nuclear exchange.[2]

Will the *fear* of such catastrophic effects by itself be enough to provide the human species a sustained lease on life? Will it continue to validate Winston Churchill's famous prophecy that in the nuclear age, "safety will be the sturdy child of terror and survival the twin brother of annihilation"?[3] Unfortunately, there is considerable cause for worry that with the spread of nuclear weapons to more and more actors around the world, the mutual deterrent relationship that evolved between the United States and the Soviet Union during the Cold War will not be replicated in the emergent Polyarchy.

It is instructive to recall that even as mutual assured destruction (MAD) capabilities matured during the Cold War, with each side capable, in the cliché of the day, of bombing the other back to the Stone Age, strategists and arms-control experts in both countries recognized that the presumed mutual deterrent balance was precarious, even terrifyingly unstable. This was because the U.S.-Soviet mutual deterrence relationship depended on a number of basic variables that could change—variables that have indeed been changing, dangerously, in today's polyarchic world.

The primary basic variable was, and is, a visible capacity of the potential victim to absorb the initial nuclear blow and effectively strike back with sufficient force to deter the nuclear aggressor in the first place. But this situation has a number of potentially volatile components. One is physical: the survivability of enough of the victim's retaliatory weapons; given the increasing cyberwar capabilities that could be employed by the aggressor to substantially disable the victim's electronically based command-and-control system, the survival of sufficient deterrent forces can no longer be taken for granted. Another variable involves identifying the aggressor, for as nuclear weapons get into the hands of nonstate as well as state actors, a potential aggressor could be able to anonymously inflict a nuclear blow on its enemy. New technologies can trace the "signatures" of detonated weapons to their country of origin, but once a weapon has found its way into the international illicit market, such information may tell nothing about the identity of those who are actually responsible for its use. Or, in the case of a geographically dispersed and mobile terrorist network, the nuclear aggressor could bank on presenting too many elusive targets in too many countries for the victim to retaliate effectively without at the same time inflicting too much collateral damage on friendly or innocent populations.

The prospect of deterring attacks with nuclear or other weapons of mass destruction also rests, optimistically, on a psychological variable: the *rationality* of the would-be aggressor—the ability to determine that the costs of a contemplated action will vastly outweigh its prospective benefits and to opt, therefore, to forgo the action. But even such rationality is subject to great variation, depending on what different people value. One person's (or culture's) highest values may be another person's (or culture's) craziness. The willing courtship of martyrdom by some jihadists in the service of their cause cannot be discounted. Nor should we fail to take into account similarly ardent strains within American culture: remember Patrick Henry's "give me liberty or give me death" declaration and the "better dead than Red" versus "better Red than dead" debate among U.S. strategists in the Cold War years.

Granting, however, that the prospect of enormous society-wide destruction will at least deter the possessors of large arsenals of nuclear weapons from "rationally" planning to use them, except in retaliation for an enemy's first use, such forbearance under the fog of war assumes a reliable psychological stability on the part of stressed commanders and decisionmakers. And that is a crucial assumption, for emotions of national pride and personal machismo could press irresistibly against rational restraint in situations where defeat looms for one's side and escalating to the nuclear level, even at the risk of mutual suicide, promises to at least reequalize the conflict. Transforming almost certain humiliation into a proverbial "game of chicken" might, by a kind of inverse logic, seem even rational—say, for a panicky government in Islamabad in a future war with India. True, such a scenario is a far cry from a full-blown world war that would threaten the survival of humankind, but looking ahead, it is not implausible to envision China and Russia and even the United States being drawn into escalating conflicts in South Asia or between different sets of nuclear-armed antagonists in the Middle East/Persian Gulf region.

Finally, there is the problem of an accidental or unauthorized use of nuclear weapons. Particularly for countries whose nuclear arsenals are smaller than their principal adversaries' or highly vulnerable to destruction on their bases, there are strong incentives to keep the nuclear facilities on high alert (ready for launching) or to increase their alert status during crises. In such conditions, the weapons are susceptible to being shot off at adversaries prematurely (while there is still a chance to avoid escalation to nuclear conflict) or on the basis of false intelligence indicating an enemy attack is under way. And paradoxically, placing one's own nuclear facilities on alert, although defensively motivated, can generate fears of an impending attack among the adversaries, provoking them to upgrade the alert status of their own systems and thereby confirming one's original fears about the onset of nuclear war. Thus, nuclear war may actually materialize not out of any intent on either side but accidentally, from the reciprocal fears of preemption. When such fears abound, the likelihood of unauthorized use by operatives somewhat below the highest levels of command can also increase. This is especially likely where high-ranking subordinates in the chain of command are aware of doctrinal or strategic debates at the highest levels concerning how to respond to an unfolding crisis: with such knowledge, they may be tempted—if they possess the keys to the arsenal, so to speak—to act on their own, convinced they are saving the nation in its moment of peril.

The probability that such nightmare scenarios will actually occur is low, but that probability must be reduced to virtually zero because of the horrendous consequences that would ensue if they ever materialized. A sanguine approach to the prospects of nuclear holocaust that leaves in place conditions that could bring it about but that are avoidable should be regarded as intolerable. We do not want to be like the man who thought he was immortal: to convince his doubting friends, he threw himself off the roof of an eighty-story skyscraper, and as he passed the fortieth floor, he told himself, "So far, so good."

What measures can be adopted to counteract the factors that could precipitate nuclear war? The prescriptions run in divergent directions. Some analysts would rely substantially on further modernizing U.S. military capabilities and employing coercive diplomacy to prevent war from escalating to the level of nuclear holocaust. Others, focusing on the likelihood of miscalculation, accidents, and irrationality under the pressures and fog of war, would disband the strategic nuclear arsenal.

Maintaining Military Primacy

With an emphasis on making sure the United States is never the object of a serious and substantial military threat from a major power, the policy of maintaining military primacy calls for sustaining a U.S. nuclear arsenal that could, in combination with conventional forces and future technological advances, unambiguously overmatch and decisively defeat in war, if it came to that, any other country's (or alliance's) military capabilities. These were the central premises of the "Nuclear Posture Review Report," issued by the Bush administration at the end of 2001. The report reiterated the U.S. intention to coordinate strategic nuclear force reductions with Russia over the coming decade. In addition, it strongly urged a major nuclear force modernization program, to include more accurate counterforce weapons. The modernization would incorporate new capabilities for destroying enemy military facilities based underground, facilities that, if buried deeply enough, presumably could not be destroyed by nonnuclear weapons.[4]

Pronouncements about such U.S. force modernization programs, even if couched in the language of arms control, are bound to perpetuate multiple-dimension arms races in the years ahead. The technologies required to enhance the survivability of the intercontinental ballistic missile (ICBM) deterrent force, to increase the effectiveness with which retaliatory blows can be delivered, to perfect early-warning systems, and to protect the U.S. population and socioeconomic infrastructure in case deterrence fails will unavoidably be seen abroad as designed to sustain U.S. war-fighting advantages—for all levels of major war, conventional or nuclear. At least Moscow and Beijing, if not others, will have a corresponding determination, reflected in their own force modernization programs, to reduce the U.S. advantages.

Even if the development of these capabilities has stemmed from a sincere motivation to prevent war and/or the escalation of war to holocaust levels with weapons of mass destruction, the ambiguous features of the capabilities—deterrent, defensive, or offensive—are liable to stimulate paranoid reactions. The dynamic is a characteristic expression of what international relations theorists call the security dilemma, whereby what one country does solely to secure its territory and people is seen by a rival country as preparation for aggression.[5] Prototypically, the security dilemma is at the core of the international controversies surrounding efforts by the United States to deploy missile defense systems around the world. Washington has assured the world that these defenses are directed only at blunting missile attacks from minor "rogue states" such as North Korea and Iran and that the limited systems are not, and do not have the capability to be, part of a full national missile defense system against the deterrent forces of Russia or China. Nonetheless, the Russians and the Chinese remain adamantly opposed to what they allege is the future "breakout" capacity of the limited missile defenses—the potential that the defenses will evolve into a more comprehensive counter to their own ICBMs.

Meanwhile, the Chinese are very actively buying, developing, and deploying advanced weapons systems.[6] The Chinese military buildup is variously interpreted in Washington. Some see it as prudent power balancing, consistent with an essentially benign grand strategy. But others see it as part of a long-term quest for regional and ultimately global military dominance, which, once attained, would allow Beijing not only to take over Taiwan with impunity but also to aggressively pursue regional and even global hegemony. Proponents of the latter, "imperialist China" interpretation focus on indications that Beijing is heavily investing in a blue-water navy that will give it an out-of-region power-projection capability (not simply more secure access to Persian Gulf and African oil). They also believe China is assiduously developing space assets with military implications.[7]

Ominously, in this partly empirical/practical, partly speculative game of competitive military buildups, the worse-case (if not worst-case) analysts tend to win out in the counsels of decision among the great powers or aspiring great powers.[8] National security advisers and military planners rarely get fired for asking for too much. (Gen. Eric Shinseki's fate after challenging Secretary of Defense Donald Rumsfeld's estimates for Operation Iraqi Freedom is a notable exception.) The military buildup advocates seldom get everything they ask for, since there are funding trade-offs with major nonmilitary programs, foreign and domestic. And proposed military budgets will sometimes be incompatible with the government's macroeconomic policy commitments (e.g., to reduce the fiscal deficit without raising new taxes). The financial constraints can translate into reductions in unnecessary military projects, but they can also produce distorted, even dangerous, strategies and force-posture modifications. The Eisenhower administration's "massive retaliation" and nuclear reliance strategies, for instance, emerged from the fiscal conservatives' push to get "more bang for the buck."[9]

It is possible that a policy of military retrenchment will be advanced by Washington in the post-Iraq, post-Afghanistan era, particularly if the principal U.S. objectives are not realized in both these conflicts. But in response to the uncertainties and frustrations of the polyarchic world—in which most countries, unable to rely on help from alliance partners or collective security institutions, are arming themselves to the teeth, it is more likely that Washington will be determined to maintain decisive U.S. military superiority over any potential adversary or combination of hostile powers. And if the United States expects that some of those foes will have weapons of mass destruction, its plans for ensuring decisive military superiority over all comers will include a robust component of nuclear weapons as well as credible plans to deploy them, if necessary, in particular contingencies, such as a threatened use of WMD against the United States.

This prospect of a WMD-armed world, with countries trapped by the security dilemma in a spiral of uncontrolled escalation of conflict, makes all too realistic the awful forecast—of low probability, it is hoped, but certainly plausible enough to stimulate corrective action—that humankind will bring on its own extinction in the absence of a fundamental break with international politics as usual. This realization has revived serious interest in the policy community in comprehensive nuclear disarmament initiatives that were previously dismissed as naively idealistic.

Nuclear Disarmament or Arms Control?

Early in the nuclear age, popular fears of a nuclear holocaust were assuaged by both the United States and the Soviet Union through schemes for general and complete disarmament that neither Washington nor Moscow considered negotiable. The United States knew that the Soviet leadership did not have the slightest intention of accepting the intrusive inspections that were a central part of the U.S. proposals, starting with the plan for international ownership of nuclear weapons and industrial processes presented to the United Nations by Bernard Baruch in 1946. (It is doubtful that the United States would, in fact, have been ready to relinquish its capabilities to a supranational apparatus even had the Soviets accepted the Baruch Plan.) And after demanding that all existing weapons and stockpiles had to be destroyed before foreigners would be allowed into the USSR to look at what was going on in that closed society, the Kremlin was hardly surprised by President Harry Truman's blunt response that under no circumstances would Americans "throw away our gun" until they were sure that others could not arm against them.[10]

For nearly two decades, the nuclear-arming superpowers persisted in this one-upmanship charade, pretending to be willing to relinquish their nuclear weapons. But with the 1962 Cuban missile crisis came the shocking recognition that they could stumble into nuclear war despite the terrible consequences both sides would suffer. As a result, the superpowers dropped the propagandistic pretense and began to engage in serious negotiations for nuclear arms *control*—that is, measures that would reinforce mutual deterrence and prevent an accidental exchange of nuclear blows or actual war caused by a miscalculation of the other's intentions.

Arms control, as distinct from disarmament, was also the objective of the intensified superpower efforts to prevent other countries from acquiring nuclear weapons—by tightening command-and-control arrangements in their respective coalitions and pressuring allies and neutrals to become parties to the nuclear Nonproliferation Treaty (NPT). A strong nonproliferation regime had become more urgent after the Cuban missile crisis as other countries—seeing that the United States and the Soviet Union had no intention of ever using nuclear weapons against one another—worried that unless they had nuclear deterrent forces of their own, they could become helpless targets of a nuclear attack in a future war. To secure the nonnuclear countries' commitment to forgo obtaining nuclear arms, the existing nuclear powers provided a quid pro quo in the form of two key promises in the NPT—which are the focus of today's nonproliferation diplomacy. The nuclear powers would help those who joined the regime to obtain the materials and technology they needed to develop peaceful nuclear energy (Articles 4 and 5). And the nuclear powers would enter into negotiations to achieve their own nuclear disarmament (Article 6).[11]

Both of these NPT provisions are complicating and frustrating efforts to prevent the spread of nuclear weapons beyond the countries that now have them (the United States, Russia, China, France, Britain, India, Pakistan, Israel, and North Korea), not only to other states but also to nonstate actors, including terrorists. The problem is that many of the nuclear materials and technologies being transferred for energy purposes under the auspices of the NPT can also be used as components in nuclear weapons programs (a dual-use ambiguity that has bedeviled efforts to distinguish between Iran's legitimate activities and those that violate its NPT obligations). But efforts by the nuclear-armed states to tighten international controls in this regard—say, by giving the International Atomic Energy Agency (IAEA) more intrusive inspection powers—run up against objections by weapons have-not nations that the United States and other nuclear powers are themselves not fulfilling their Article 6 commitments for their own nuclear disarmament. Moreover, the nuclear powers have, in the meantime, let India and Pakistan into the nuclear weapons club, imposing only minimum sanctions on them, and they are transferring nuclear weapons and technologies to these countries for their energy programs with less stringent controls than are imposed on the NPT member governments.

These disturbing realities threaten to undermine and collapse the nonproliferation regime at a time when there are more and more incentives—given the undependability of collective security arrangements in the Polyarchy—for countries large and small and political movements as well to provide for their own defense. And increasingly, that means acquiring the most lethal capabilities possible.

The ominous prospect of a Hobbesian world bristling with nuclear weapons is creating new audiences among policy influentials for ambitious nuclear disarmament proposals. Ideas that prominent nuclear weapons abolitionists such as Jonathan Schell have been promoting for decades are now receiving at least a respectful hearing even among Traditional Realists.[12]

One sign of the times is the call for a nuclear weapons–free planet by former secretaries of state George P. Shultz and Henry A. Kissinger, former secretary of defense William J. Perry, and the former chair of the Senate Arms Services Committee, Sam Nunn. That call was announced in their article entitled "A World Free of Nuclear Weapons," which appeared in the *Wall Street Journal* on January 4, 2007. Urging the countries possessing nuclear weapons to agree upon and begin implementing a set of "urgent steps that would lay the groundwork for a world free of the nuclear threat," they proposed a starting package that included:

- Increasing the warning time on deployed nuclear weapons to reduce the danger of their accidental or unauthorized use;
- Continuing to reduce the size of existing nuclear arsenals;
- Eliminating short-range nuclear weapons designed to be forward deployed;
- Getting the United States and other holdout countries to ratify the Comprehensive Test Ban Treaty;
- Ensuring the highest standards of security for all stocks of nuclear weapons, weapons-usable plutonium, and highly enriched uranium;
- Strengthening international controls on the uranium-enrichment process; and
- Halting the production of fissile material.[13]

The authors also called for new and enhanced efforts to resolve conflicts that induce nations to acquire and brandish nuclear weapons. But other than admonishing countries, including the United States, to dispense with nuclear-centered diplomacy, their op-ed article provided no transformative political prescriptions for how to conduct, or even phase in, such diplomacy in parallel with movement toward the goal of a world free of nuclear weapons. Nonetheless, coming as it did from four individuals who, in their previous official roles, had reputations for hawkishness regarding the connections between force and diplomacy, the article created quite a stir among international security experts

around the world. If Henry Kissinger and his cohorts were now joining the ranks of the nuclear abolitionists, perhaps some of the people
in "serious" think tanks and on military planning staffs—those whose
knee-jerk reaction would be to consider such a call naively uninformed
about world realities—needed to revise their own thinking.

To be sure, the political and technical difficulties in achieving and sustaining total nuclear disarmament are as daunting as ever, perhaps even
more so. But strategically sophisticated abolitionists claim the obstacles
are not insurmountable. And more important still, they argue that a
failure to turn the world in this direction will, year by year, substantially
increase the likelihood of nuclear wars with immediate and long-term
effects drastically disruptive of the environmental, socioeconomic, and
political requirements for the healthy survival of the human species.

Some fear that denuclearizing the arsenals of the United States and
other responsible powers will undermine their ability to deter and defend
against threats to their own and international peace and security by rogue
states and other irresponsible actors, including terrorist-supporting states.
But the nuclear abolitionists (who are not arguing for general disarmament) point to the superior nonnuclear military capabilities that will still
be retained by the responsible powers. They also argue that the global
outlawing and dismantling of nuclear weapons will deprive aggressors
of the "great equalizer"—or counterdeterrent—function that the less
powerful can hope to exercise with even an inferior arsenal of nuclear
weapons because of their vast destructive effects.

But does not such a no-nuclear-weapons regime, especially if it includes countries that were hoping to exploit the great equalizer effect,
require a degree of international verification and intrusive inspection that
most such nations would not want to accept? Jonathan Schell's answer
typifies the kind of outside-the-box thinking that the abolitionists believe
is required to obtain such a regime. According to Schell, an omnibus
and combined disarmament/nonproliferation negotiating process would
be convened in which the United States and the other major nuclear-
armed states would agree to give up their own nuclear bombs in return
for one guarantee: the other states would have to accept strict, verifiable,

fully inspectable, and reliably enforceable measures to ensure that all countries honor their commitments not to possess nuclear weapons or weapons-production facilities and not to transfer such capabilities to non-governmental groups. As Schell put it, "The nuclear arsenals of the great powers would be the largest pile of bargaining chips ever brought to any negotiating table." He envisioned an incremental process of bargaining in which, for example, Russia and the United States would reduce their nuclear weapons down to a few hundred each and ratify the Comprehensive Test Ban Treaty in exchange for the nuclear weapons–free states' surrender of their rights to the troublesome nuclear fuel cycle. Further reductions, also by the other nuclear powers, could follow in return for the institution of inspections of increasing severity and intrusiveness, leading eventually to the final abolition of nuclear arms.[14]

Indicative of the new willingness among international security experts to devote some brainpower to fresh analysis, rather than dismissive criticism of such proposals, the International Institute for Strategic Studies (IISS), with support from the British government, launched a major research study in the summer of 2007 on what a commitment to a world free of nuclear weapons would mean in practice. Those associated with the IISS project suggested that "the aim of the study would not be to establish or advocate a programme of action, but simply to lay a better foundation of understanding upon which debate about prospects and options might be advanced."[15]

One of the most vexing problems would be how to deal with those states or nonstate entities that, either openly or clandestinely, are determined to remain outside the no-nuclear-weapons regime. Shell's reaction to this prospect left something to be desired. He invoked the historical record, arguing that since Hiroshima and Nagasaki, nuclear-armed states have refrained from actually using their nuclear weapons in war, even against enemies lacking a nuclear retaliatory capability, because their leaders have understood that such use "would surely have occasioned worldwide disgust, horror, fury—that the world and posterity would have branded the user a pariah, an enemy of humanity, criminally insane."[16] But this argument ignores those cases—not at all fanciful—in which the possessors of WMD are so convinced of the righteousness of their cause that it is worth whatever excoriation they may suffer on earth, and even death if necessary, to exterminate their enemies, especially if this will gain them blessings in heaven. I will return to this concern in the following chapter on reducing the role of force in world politics.

Meanwhile, the prospect of weapons of mass destruction getting into the hands of the "wrong" people is an appropriate urgent concern for the U.S. and other governments. So let me discuss briefly the so-called loose-nukes problem.

Preventing Terrorism with WMD

The prevention of acts of war involving the catastrophic destruction of humans and property requires more than states negotiating and adhering to treaties outlawing or limiting the possession and use of weapons of mass destruction. It also requires that nongovernmental and nonaccountable groups do not gain access to the proscribed lethal materials and technology, through either illicit transfers or theft. To prevent terrorists or others from gaining illegal access to deactivated or dismantled WMD and to potential WMD-related materials in ostensibly peaceful research and fabricating facilities, initiatives have been adopted by the United States and other governments to secure and/or eliminate such WMD components. The best known of these is the Cooperative Nuclear Threat Reduction Program, established in 1992 (popularly known as Nunn-Lugar after its two major legislative sponsors, Senators Sam Nunn and Richard Lugar). This program was mandated "to secure and dismantle weapons of mass destruction and their associated infrastructure in the former Soviet Union states."[17] Accordingly, Nunn-Lugar established the framework through which funds and expertise have been provided to Russia, Ukraine, Georgia, Azerbaijan, Uzbekistan, and Kazakhstan for the decommissioning of nuclear, biological, and chemical weapon stockpiles, as provided for in various U.S.-Soviet arms-limitation treaties. Coupled with Nunn-Lugar and various multilateral undertakings, such as the Global Threat

Reduction Initiative in 2004, a large effort has been launched to also secure or destroy weapons-related materials, particularly highly enriched uranium (HEU) and separated plutonium, that are associated with peaceful nuclear research and power facilities in countries party to the NPT.

Despite such initiatives, an authoritative assessment by the Project on Managing the Atom at Harvard University's Belfer Center for Science and International Affairs concluded in 2007 that "the essential ingredients of nuclear weapons exist in over 40 countries, and there are scores of sites that are not secure enough to defeat the capabilities that terrorists and criminals have demonstrated." Under Nunn-Lugar, impressive progress has been made in Russia, which has the largest stockpile of nuclear weapons and materials in the world. But the project assessment points to continuing vulnerabilities to theft, warning that "less than a hundredth of one percent of Russia's vast stockpile of weapons-usable nuclear materials would be enough for several terrorist nuclear bombs." Moreover, outside the former Soviet Union, efforts to improve nuclear security are still in their early stages, and "only a small fraction of the HEU-fueled research reactor sites have yet had all their HEU removed."[18]

Intensified efforts under the Global Threat Reduction Initiative and beefed-up capabilities under the Proliferation Security Initiative for detecting and interdicting illegal transshipments across borders and at sea may reduce the likelihood of catastrophic terrorist attacks, but they cannot eliminate the prospect of such horrendous events materializing. Bringing the probabilities closer to zero will also require progress in reducing the role of force in world politics—the world interest that is the subject of the following chapter.

Arresting Global Warming

Not all of the consequences of global warming, including the projected flooding of coastal areas, are expected to directly threaten the healthy survival of the entire human species. Some regions of the globe and some communities will suffer more than others; indeed, in some places, the warmer temperatures could increase agricultural productivity or allow for the mining and extraction of natural resources (including oil), previously precluded because of year-round ice cover. But if the projections of the Intergovernmental Panel on Climate Change (IPCC) are essentially correct, with respect to both the rate of increase in the planet's average temperature and its impacts on global climatic and weather patterns, the severe ecological disturbances experienced in many areas and their disruptive effects on human habitats would have ominous implications for the continued health and well-being of people worldwide.

The latest IPCC assessment reflects a consensus among the more than 200 scientists appointed by the World Meteorological Organization and the United Nations Environment Program about the threat of global warming. It was reviewed by additional panels of independent scientists and relevant agencies in the sponsoring nations (including the United States) before its publication in 2007. Assuming it will be business as usual on Earth (meaning there will be no fundamental abatement of the emissions contributing to the so-called greenhouse effect), the IPCC assessment includes the following forecasts:

- A continuing reduction in the availability of water in areas normally supplied by meltwater from major mountain ranges (affecting more than one-sixth of the world's population);
- Millions of people flooded every year by the 2080s because of sea-level rise, caused mainly by melting glaciers—with the megadeltas of Asia and Africa as well as small islands having the largest numbers of people affected;
- Unprecedented intensity and frequency of ecosystem and climatic disturbances—hurricanes, tsunamis, floods, droughts, wildfires, and defoliation by insects;
- Encroachment of deserts into previously fertile croplands;
- Progressive acidification of the oceans; and
- Increased risk of extinction for 20 to 30 percent of plant and animal species.

The devastating implications for the health of perhaps a billion people around the globe, particularly those in poorer communities with low adaptive capacities, are elaborated in the IPCC studies. They include increases in malnutrition and its attendant disorders; more deaths, diseases (particularly diarrhea), and injuries due to heat waves, floods, storms, fires, and droughts; a greater frequency of cardiorespiratory problems due to higher concentrations of ground-level ozone; and an altered spatial distribution of infectious disease vectors, making for a higher probability of epidemics and pandemics.[19]

Since most of the bad effects are projected to occur in the poorest areas of the globe, why should Realists (even Higher Realists) be all that exercised about global warming? Why should the United States and other countries in the least affected Northern Hemisphere zones distort their economies now with stringent regulations on carbon emissions and huge government subsidies for alternative (non-fossil-fuel) energy projects instead of dealing amelioratively, on a case-by-case basis, with the not-so-terrible effects as they gradually materialize in the future? These questions reflect an inadequate recognition of the extent to which there are two sides to the presumably positive coin of globalization. On one side, there are the tremendous benefits enjoyed by the United States as a result of the increasing transnational mobility of goods, money, and information; on the other side, there are the problems caused by the increasing porousness of national borders with respect to climatic, material, and ideational carriers of socially disruptive and debilitating phenomena.

Yes, the impacts of the planet's destabilized climate, such as floods, hurricanes, tsunamis, desertification, water shortages, and pestilence, will probably be most directly and initially felt by poor and vulnerable communities. But the extreme stress this will put on the societies and states in those areas—hordes of starving and homeless migrants, the out-break of infectious diseases not susceptible to quarantine, the breakdown of already thinly capable essential public services—will provide highly combustible conditions for violent intrastate and transstate conflicts that can easily escalate into regionwide conflagrations. The United States and other well-off countries, with substantial investments in these regions, will not be able to simply absorb or ignore the costs of the widespread breakdown in public order, but the prospects for successful intervention may now be extremely low. The resulting multiplication of failed and failing states that are unable to minister to the basic needs of the affected people will leave the world with vast ungoverned areas up for grabs by demagogues and terrorist movements. And both demagogues and terrorists feed on such chaos and the anger of suffering peoples against those who are alleged to have been the cause of their misery, including the United States.[20]

Such scenarios of suffering and mayhem initially concentrated in local areas are based upon the more conservative and least alarmist IPCC forecasts of the pace and magnitude of global warming. If the more extreme models are used to project the emerging climate conditions, massive physical, socioeconomic, and political impacts analogous to those forecast for the most vulnerable areas could also be felt directly in the United States and other advanced industrial countries.

Measures that have a reasonable chance of arresting the global warming before it progresses to catastrophic levels are expensive. Some of the most crucial ones are sure to be opposed by industry groups whose economic and political powers flow from the dependence of most industrial and industrializing societies on fossil fuels—the prime source of the carbon emissions that are contributing to the greenhouse effect. But as a major study of the economic problems, commissioned by the British government, concluded, "The benefits of strong and early action far outweigh the economic costs of not acting."[21] The *Stern Review* (named after its principal author, economist Sir Nicolas Stern) estimated that "if we don't act, the overall costs and risks of climate change will be equivalent to losing at least 5% of global GDP [gross domestic product] each year, now and forever. If a wider range of risks and impacts is taken into account, the estimates of damage could rise to 20% of GDP or more." In contrast, the *Review* calculated, "the costs of action—reducing greenhouse gas emissions to avoid the worst aspects of climate change—can be limited to around 1% of global GDP each year."[22]

In endorsing the *Stern Review* and making stabilizing the climate a centerpiece of both its domestic and foreign policies, the British government argued that the world did not have to choose between averting climate change and promoting growth and development: emissions could be cut through increased energy efficiency, changes in demand, and the adoption of clean sources of power. Although the power sector around the world would need to be "decarbonated" by at least 60 percent by 2050 and deep cuts would also be required in the transportation sector, fossil fuels could still make up over half of the global energy supply.

To accomplish these climate-stabilization goals, the *Stern Review* outlined a set of policy initiatives (and the British government has become a global champion of this advice). Absolutely required is an increase in the price of carbon, achieved through a combination of taxes, trading schemes, and regulation. Also necessary is a major program to support innovation and the deployment of low-carbon technologies. Then there is the need to curb deforestation, since the loss of natural forests around the world contributes more to greenhouse emissions than the transportation sector does. And finally, countries around the world must act collectively to provide the global public good of a stabilized climate. But this last requirement, which is an essential condition for the fulfillment of the other policy imperatives, has not been materializing to the degree that it must because the three largest contributors to the carbon buildup dangerously enveloping the planet—the United States, China, and India—have resisted the idea of making a binding commitment to reduce their emissions.

I will return to the crucial importance of generating international collective action to deal with environmental threats in a later chapter. For now, I want to emphasize that until this aspect of Higher Realism is integrated into U.S. foreign policy, many of the other world and national interests cannot be adequately secured.

Reducing the Role of Force
in World Politics

Higher Realism challenges the presumably realistic aphorism that force is the *ultima ratio* of international politics as well as the cynical formula that might makes right. Force—physical compulsion—may often be the *proxima* (immediate and temporary) determinant of who gets what when there is a conflict of interests and wills, but rarely is it the ultimate determinant. More often than not, arrangements established and maintained primarily by force lack durability because they breed resentment as to their legitimacy, which leads to their ultimate undoing. Nor can there be durability to arrangements constructed on the premise that what is legitimate (or right) attaches only to what those in power have been able to enforce and what the people have been force-fed to accept. Well-functioning communities depend mostly on the uncoerced acceptance by their members of community rules and mores, with the use of force to induce compliance being a necessary exception rather than the norm.

In today's world, reducing the role of force—its marginalization, definitely not its embrace as a normal tool of statecraft—is particularly in the interest of countries heavily involved in global commerce, since war typically disrupts the international exchange of goods, services, and money as well as travel and communication. This is certainly true for the United States—contrary to the Marxist myth that the corporate sector, which benefits from arms production and sales, is the driving force behind U.S. foreign policy. Of course, firms that primarily live off of arms contracts may indeed look with favor upon Pentagon budgets featuring multibillion-dollar outlays for weapons research and development and production. But the largest multinational and multiproduct firms (many of which also produce big-ticket military items) have been in the forefront of lobbying efforts to reduce tensions and open up commerce with adversaries (with China and the Soviet Union during the Cold War and, more recently, with Vietnam and Cuba and even Iran and North Korea). There are occasions when, to protect free international commerce and its other interests, the United States must be prepared to use force, but more fundamentally, the country has a vital national interest in reducing the role of force in world politics.

What, then, does the national-cum-world interest in reducing the role of force entail? First, the United States, as the most powerfully armed country on earth, must itself take the lead in de-emphasizing the role of force—particularly *preventive* war—as an instrument of its foreign policy. Washington needs to show, not only in its rhetoric but also by its actions, that it adheres to the core "Just War" constraints on the resort to force and the conduct of military operations. Simultaneously, it should recommit itself to substantially reducing the weapons of mass destruction in the U.S. arsenal—not just preventing other countries from obtaining such weapons. As the world's leading arms supplier, the United States also needs to get serious about drastically constricting both the legal and illicit markets in weapons. While de-emphasizing the coercive aspects of carrot-and-stick diplomacy and pursuing arms control, U.S. statecraft should be taking the lead in incorporating and enhancing processes and institutions for dispute resolution and conflict control, including intraconflict and postconflict peacekeeping and peace-building operations—privileging these wherever possible over strategies that feature the threat and use of force.

Decreasing the Decibel Level in U.S. Strategic Pronouncements

The perception around the world, and at home, that the United States has been conducting a militarized diplomacy is the product of official public policy pronouncements as well as of the country's deployments and interventions. Although prudential statecraft, including Higher Realism, grants the need to maintain a capacity to deter and defend against probable threats to the country's security and well-being, it rarely requires that center stage be given to frightful scenarios of such threats and loud declamations of the military strategies for countering them. Today, more than ever before, Theodore Roosevelt's famous counsel to "speak softly and carry a large stick" is sage advice—at least with regard to the vocalization. How large and what kind of a stick are matters for additional special reflection.

In the immediate aftermath of the 9/11 terrorist attack, angry rhetoric from the president and cabinet-level officials was warranted, although the general public was ready, with or without rousing speeches from on high, to support vigorous counteraction—such as the invasion of Afghanistan to depose the Al Qaeda–harboring Taliban regime. But the rationale subsequently issued by the Bush administration for Operation Enduring Freedom in Afghanistan and impending future actions (such as Operation Iraqi Freedom) in the president's *National Security Strategy of the United States* went too far. That rationale needs to be substantially modulated, if not substantively revised.

Issued under the name of President George W. Bush, the 2002 strategy paper averred that in countering "rogue states" and "terrorists who seek martyrdom in death," the United States "can no longer rely solely on a reactive posture as we have in the past," especially "traditional concepts of deterrence." The magnitude of the potential harm—acts of terror, possibly involving the use of weapons of mass destruction—established the case for "taking anticipatory action to defend ourselves, even if uncertainty remains as to the time and place of the enemy's attack. To forestall or prevent such hostile acts by our adversaries, the United States will, if necessary, act preemptively."[1]

The administration's argument against relying mainly on deterrence to combat terrorism—that deterrence presumes a rational enemy—was persuasive. So was the military argument that striking preemptively could prevent or limit the damage to the United States. And the strategy paper was also correct in pointing out that international law allowed that "nations need not suffer an attack before they can lawfully take action to defend themselves against forces that present an imminent danger of attack." But in using the term *preemption* to cover military action in anticipation of enemy attacks that were not yet imminent—in other words, to conflate preemption with preventive war—the administration was openly proclaiming a grand strategy that did directly contradict the prohibitions on military aggression that had been evolving in mainline international law. And coming from the government of the United States—an erstwhile champion of these prohibitions—the new doctrine and actions taken in its name (such as Operation Iraqi Freedom) could be regarded by other nations as a precedent, legitimizing the use of force as a normal instrument of foreign policy.

One way of reversing the retrograde setback to the world and national interest in reducing the role of force would be to follow Teddy Roosevelt's admonition. In the present context, this would mean that planning for situations in which the United States might be compelled to preemptively or preventively initiate war should not be elevated to the level of publicly articulated grand strategy; nor should these extreme options be talked about as if they were the essence of U.S. policy. Another way would be to reaffirm the core principles of the Just War tradition publicly and in actual national security planning and to adapt them to the current polyarchic realities.

Acceptance of Just War Constraints

The Just War tradition,[2] the predominant moral discourse on the international use of force—taught in the United States in the military academies of all the services—comprises a body of principles that flow from two fundamental propositions: (1) the country's fighting forces should not be ordered into combat unless the decision to do so can satisfy a number of stringent criteria as to the war's legality, morality, and prudence, and (2) when engaged in combat, the country's fighting forces should not inflict more destruction and pain on the enemy than is militarily necessary, and every possible effort should be made to avoid harming people who are not part of the enemy's fighting forces.[3]

Adherence to the first proposition would require the United States, in its official rhetoric and behavior, to keep the threshold between nonviolent diplomacy and war thick and clear, recognizing that war can easily get out of hand, inflicting irreversible damage on the belligerent nations and overwhelming the political purposes for which they took up arms. Accordingly, in all brink-of-war crises, the government would structure its decisionmaking process to ensure a thoroughgoing assessment of whether the interests and values at stake are of sufficient weight—and have sufficient support in the country—to warrant going to war; it would also carefully assess whether resorting to military force will better serve the interests at stake than will nonmilitary actions. As a part of any prewar "moment of truth" calculation of the costs versus benefits of a contemplated military operation, the president would demand an analysis of what it will take to restore at least minimal civic life where it has been severely disrupted by the war to which the United States is a party.

I do not recommend that the United States abjure going to war when the use of military force is clearly needed to secure the country's irreducible national interests. Nor am I recommending that the United States should never use force on behalf of the security and well-being of other people or the advancement of world order. I am arguing, however, that when it comes to military intervention or international peacekeeping missions, the burden of justification lies with those who are urging the United States to employ its lethal power.

On the issue of military intervention for reasons other than U.S. national security or to counter clear and present threats to international peace and security, ethicist Michael Walzer, adapting a formulation developed by the British philosopher John Stuart Mill, provides a set of useful restrictive criteria. At least one of the following three conditions, Walzer argues, must be present to legitimize military intervention by outside powers into the territory of another country: (1) a full-scale military struggle is under way within the country over the nature of the polity and who will rule; (2) the country's borders have already been crossed by foreign forces, so that what is now at issue is counterintervention; or (3) the violation of human rights within the country is so egregious (for example, genocide or large-scale ethnic cleansing) that the national government has forfeited its normal sovereignty rights.[4]

These criteria should not be taken as sufficient causes for military intervention; rather, they indicate the kinds of conditions that must be present if a country is to override the crucial world-order norm against initiating interstate war. Even when such conditions are present, military intervention would not be justified unless it also satisfied other widely endorsed Just War criteria—namely:

- *Last resort*—every nonmilitary option for dealing with the situation has been explored, and there are persuasive grounds for concluding that the other measures will fail;
- *Proportional means*—the scale, duration, and intensity of the proposed military action will be at the minimum level necessary to deal with the situation; and
- *Balance of consequences*—there is a high likelihood of the military action succeeding in dealing with the situation, and the consequences of such action are not likely to be worse than the consequences of inaction.[5]

If war is undertaken after all these considerations have been seriously weighed, the second fundamental Just War proposition mandates that the fighting should be as constrained as possible, not only by meeting the proportionality and balance-of-consequences criteria but also by specifically making sure that the lives of innocent people (noncombatants, civilians) are spared.

The principle of noncombatant immunity, severely eroded in the city-bombing strategies of World War II, has since been enshrined in numerous conventions to which the United States is a party. And it has been quite conscientiously applied to constrain regular U.S. military operations. But to the extent that "irregular" forces are employed against U.S. combat units in insurgencies—sometimes deliberately disguised as civilians—it has proven difficult to uphold.

Some military strategists have hoped that the Revolution in Military Affairs, in particular the dramatic improvements in accurate targeting and precision delivery of ordnance, would reduce the amount of unwanted "collateral damage" inflicted in military operations. Paradoxically, however, the technological innovations have made it easier to go to war, on the assumption that what is transpiring on the battlefield can be more tightly reined in to conform to the political objectives and strategies of national command authorities. And the hope of again being able to use technologically transformed warfare as an instrument of foreign policy (Operation Iraqi Freedom being exhibit A) has itself proven to be an illusion, for less technologically advanced adversaries have adapted accordingly with their own asymmetric strategies and tactics, such as using civilians as human shields, carrying out suicide bombings, and using various other forms of terrorism. Despite the difficulties, however—indeed, because of them—once deadly conflict starts and the fog of war envelops the battlefield, it is imperative to resist the temptation to throw away the moral and legal rule books prohibiting the targeting of noncombatants and the destruction of civilian facilities.

Unfortunately, the widening of the spectrum of military conflict, from strategies and weapons of precision (and even nonlethality), at one end, to weapons of mass destruction, on the other, does not augur well for either reducing the likelihood of war or controlling the dimensions of violence once war starts. The inherent volatility and unpredictability of contemporary war and its consequences across an enormous range of destruction make it all the more imperative to keep military operations as means of last resort and not to normalize them as an instrument of statecraft.

Disarmament, Arms Limitation, and Arms Control

The National Rifle Association's favorite aphorism—"Guns don't kill people, people kill people"—is a half-truth and no more than a half-truth. The reality is that the quantity, quality, and deployment of arms sported by governments and people around the world can significantly affect the propensity of conflicts turning violent and escalating to higher levels of violence.

It may be true that if all the missiles, bombs, artillery, and handheld guns were eliminated, humans would revert back to spears, swords, and knives to prosecute their conflicts. But even if the sources of violent conflict lie deep in the human psyche and in societal conditions, the fact is that when political adversaries and others decide to go to war and adopt particular fighting strategies, their decisions are profoundly affected by what kinds and levels of lethal combat capabilities they possess.

Thus, the nuclear "balance of terror" between the United States and the Soviet Union played a crucial part in preventing the Cold War from erupting into a U.S.-Soviet hot war. As Winston Churchill put it in his famous aphorism about safety being the sturdy child of terror, the way to avoid war was for it to be as horrible as possible—for *both* sides, so there could be no winner.[6] To ensure this mutual deterrent effect, the United States and the Soviet Union felt compelled to institutionalize their respective capabilities to devastate one another no matter who struck first—that is, to provide for mutual assured destruction (MAD)—in a set of strategic arms–limitation treaties and accords. A centerpiece of MAD, the antiballistic missile (ABM) treaty signed by Richard Nixon

84

and Leonid Brezhnev in 1972, was designed to prevent either side from deploying weapons that could intercept and destroy a substantial portion of the other's offensive ballistic missiles, thus weakening its assured destruction capability.

President Ronald Reagan attempted to break out of the mutual nuclear hostage relationship, which he branded immoral, by calling for the development of a nationwide defense against strategic attack, his Strategic Defense Initiative (SDI). Dubbed Star Wars by journalists because key interceptors were to be based in outer space, the SDI was opposed by the Soviets, many other governments, and most U.S. arms-control experts, who doubted its feasibility but believed it was nevertheless subversive of mutual deterrence. However, Reagan and Mikhail Gorbachev, the Soviet leader, were able to negotiate an important strategic arms–control measure, the Intermediate Nuclear Force (INF) Treaty eliminating all U.S. and Soviet missiles with ranges between 500 and 3,000 miles that were deployed in or targeted on the European theater. This breakthrough limited disarmament pact, which led to subsequent agreements reducing the size of U.S. and Soviet intercontinental strategic arsenals, was a centerpiece of the diplomacy ending the Cold War. The INF Treaty validated the wisdom of the arms controllers that just as an arms race is a symptom of an underlying political conflict, the way in which it is conducted or turned off can crucially affect the nature of the political conflict itself.

Currently and in the near future, then, what arms programs of the United States, and of countries whose arms programs can be influenced by the United States, should be the focus of efforts to reduce the role of force in world politics?

WMD Limits

Of greatest importance, as indicated in the previous chapter, are the weapons of mass destruction, which, if used, could threaten the healthy survival of the human species. However, the fact that nuclear weapons were not used during the Cold War and probably did, as Churchill argued, discourage the United States and the Soviet Union from going to war against each other (but not from supporting and fighting proxy wars) has been invoked by some statespersons to justify their own countries' continued possession of at least "minimum deterrent" nuclear arsenals. A few strategic theorists have even inferred from the U.S.-Soviet mutual deterrent relationship that the whole world would be more stable— that is, less pervaded by war—if most countries had their own nuclear weapons.[7] Despite the logical and historical weakness of the stability-through-proliferation speculation, comprehensive nuclear disarmament proposals must contend against (1) the reluctance of any of the existing nuclear-armed states (the United States, Russia, China, France, Britain, India, Pakistan, and Israel) to dispense with their trump card, and (2) the determination of many others (not just North Korea and Iran) to retain at least a live option to develop or obtain nuclear arms.

Even if the United States and Russia were to fulfill their standing commitments to reduce their strategic nuclear weapons to approximately 2,000 (down from the estimated 6,000 they now retain), it is doubtful that any of the other nuclear-armed countries would agree to reduce their strategic nuclear forces by a comparable percentage. More likely, they would be stimulated to build up their arsenals, thereby moving within reach of closing the gap that separates them from the two leading nuclear powers.

A more fruitful approach to arresting the proliferation of nuclear weapons would be to radically de-emphasize the importance of all WMD in U.S. grand strategy as well as their political worth for any country in terms of international diplomacy. The United States does not need to employ nuclear, chemical, biological, or enhanced radiation weapons to conduct whatever military missions will plausibly be needed to secure U.S. national interests in the foreseeable future. Issuing threats to use such weapons as a stratagem of coercive diplomacy would be a confession of moral and political bankruptcy, something the United States clearly would want to avoid; if others should make such threats, the appropriate response would be to expose the weakness that drives them to this extreme rather than to imitate them.

There is no need to emulate the city-busting strategies of World War II, which subsequent strategic analysis shows were not, as popularly believed, what induced either Germany or Japan to surrender.[8] All militarily or economically critical targets can be more efficiently destroyed, disabled, or captured, while minimizing civilian casualties, with weapons of precise (not mass) destruction.[9] Nor are there morally acceptable—or practical—reasons for threatening to use weapons of mass destruction against an enemy in order to deter a WMD attack on the United States. The needed deterrence against such an attack is best provided by survivable second-strike capabilities, sufficient to hobble the military power of the aggressor. But if, horrendously, deterrence fails and the United States falls victim to a mass-destruction attack, there is no strategically compelling reason to compound the horror instead of retaliating against the remaining military power of the enemy.

This strategic assessment means that the United States, without compromising its usable military prowess, can and should promote not a no-*first-use*-of-WMD regime but a *no-use*-of-WMD regime. Ideally, all WMD-capable countries would join with the United States in committing never to use the weapons. But such a commitment still makes sense for the United States even if others are unwilling to forgo the use of or threat to use WMD. The United States and most other countries have already ratified bans on producing and using chemical and biological weapons: the Chemical Weapons Convention (CWC) and the Biological Weapons Convention (which needs some tightening of its loose language). But Washington has not been enthusiastic about a comparable ban on the use, let along the production, of nuclear weapons.

It no longer makes strategic sense for the United States to insist on keeping nuclear weapons in the arsenal as either an explicit or an implicit deterrent to any attempt by the Soviets and/or the Chinese to take advantage of their various quantitative advantages for combat against the United States and its allies on the Eurasian mainland. Nonetheless, there remains a strong consensus in the policy community in favor of maintaining U.S. nuclear superiority over the Russians, the Chinese, and any possible combination of anti-U.S. nuclear powers—thus the U.S.

failure as yet to ratify the Comprehensive Test Ban Treaty for nuclear weapons. (The thinking is that testing might be needed to make sure the U.S. nuclear arsenal continues to be impressive enough to deter any future nuclear-armed adversary from escalating to nuclear war.) Among the nuclear weapons that would presumably be important for this purpose would be earth penetrators capable of destroying enemy strategic weapons deployed deep underground. Skeptics point out, however, that these bunker busters could accomplish this counterforce purpose only if the locations of most of the deep underground weapons were known, and for such targets, enhanced conventional weaponry and/or special forces could probably do the job almost as well.[10] For such an uncertain marginal advantage, which would only exist in the rarest of scenarios, the United States would be perpetuating the kind of nuclearized strategy that the new strategic wisdom should consider obsolete.

Reining in Arms Transfers

The interest in reducing the role of force in world politics is frustrated by the runaway transfer of arms—mostly through sales—from the major arms-producing countries to governments and insurgent movements in the developing world. The burgeoning number of eager buyers and sellers (with deals totaling approximately $160 billion annually in recent years) reflects the post–Cold War reduction in superpower control over allies and clients in the emergent Polyarchy and the dramatic increase in politically autonomous and rivalrous actors.

Not surprisingly, the leading sellers are the United States and Russia, each having built up huge arms-producing sectors for balancing one another's power around the world during the Cold War. Currently, in a typical year, the United States negotiates over 40 percent of the dollar value of all such deals, and Russia negotiates over 20 percent, with France, Britain, China, Germany, and Italy following in that order.[11]

Among the ranking arms sellers, the United States has been the most selective with respect to buyers since the end of the Cold War, consistent with its aspiration to be the hegemonic leader of the international system. And it has been critical of the others for cultivating developing-country clients regardless of how those clients might use the weapons domestically or against their neighbors. However, such complaints are not sufficient to arrest the expanding market.

Although France and Britain have been active in negotiating arms-transfer arrangements with their former colonies and although Russia and China have attempted to preserve a dominant supplier status with their former Cold War allies, none of these nations have been hesitant to compete for clients in the others' erstwhile spheres of influence. Russia and China, for example, are very active hawkers of arms all over Africa and Latin America, with the still professedly Marxist China imposing no ideological litmus tests for determining appropriate commercial partners. Similarly, Britain and France are active arms merchants in Central Asia, an area of Soviet control during the Cold War and a venue for intense Anglo-Russian rivalry in previous eras.

By contrast, under the administration of George W. Bush (considerably more so than under Bill Clinton or the elder Bush), the United States has played favorites and discriminated against other potential arms recipients according to their support for U.S. counterterrorism operations and their willingness to cooperate with U.S. opposition to the International Criminal Court. And there has been a persisting geopolitical cast to major U.S. arms transfers to countries in various regions to help them balance one another's military powers—Israel vis-à-vis Egypt and/or Saudi Arabia and, increasingly, India vis-à-vis Pakistan and China. But these politicized arms-transfer policies are sustaining self-perpetuating and intensifying regional arms races that raise the demand for more and more expensive lethal equipment. Such races may be satisfying to the competing suppliers, but they work against prospects for a nonviolent resolution of the local conflicts.

As the leading arms supplier, the United States is in a position to spearhead a turnaround in what has become a mindless fueling of arms races and their attendant conflicts. To exert such leadership, however, Washington must be willing not only to sacrifice considerable foreign exchange earnings but also to demand, as a high-priority world interest, that other major arms suppliers exercise similar restraint.

Conflict Moderation

There is merit to efforts designed to regulate the global market in weapons, to limit the size and characteristics of arsenals, and to gain acceptance of legal and moral principles that delegitimize war for other than the most necessary and profound causes and constrain belligerents from using disproportionate violence during war. When pragmatically and flexibly promoted by the United States in ways that credibly establish the country's willingness to constrain its own military programs and strategies in order to serve the world interest in reducing the role of force, such initiatives can induce emulation by others. But only so much can be accomplished at this essentially military level. Substantial progress toward a less war-prone world requires increased reliance on and enhancement of processes and institutions for the nonviolent prosecution and resolution of disputes. And in order to induce others to moderate their behavior, the United States must participate in and rely upon such processes and institutions more actively than it has done in recent years.

The processes and institutions for nonviolent handling of international disputes range across a spectrum from standard bilateral or multilateral negotiations to subjugation to the findings of supranational organizations. Along this spectrum, countries give up increasing amounts of their sovereignty—which is something the United States, in its own interest and in the world interest, will have to begin to do.

The Art of Negotiation

There is a growing body of literature on how to succeed in negotiation, much of it produced by experienced negotiators in the private sector. These works show negotiation to be an art form, which, if applied with skill in international diplomacy, can do much to steer countries off of a collision course. Successful negotiation requires that the parties be able to distinguish their secondary interests from their primary (or vital) interests and also willing to compromise on their secondary interests; such abilities were crucial for resolving the Cuban missile crisis.[12] In a bargaining sequence, a skillful negotiator knows when and how to communicate such interest priorities without weakening a party's bargaining position. Being adept at discovering the relevant interest priorities of one's opponent is also important in a negotiation to back away from the brink of war. Without such empathy, a miscalculation of how much the other can be challenged is likely, as is a dangerous misperception as to when an opponent's threat to use force is real or only a bluff.[13]

The toolbox of negotiating techniques to defuse potentially explosive crises also includes the stratagem of fractionating disputes into discrete issues, separating out the negotiable issues from the nonnegotiable ones. This does not preclude linking, judiciously and when the time is ripe, an outcome the opponent now eagerly wants to other outcomes that were previously nonstarters. Such fractionating followed by linking was a feature of Henry Kissinger's step-by-step diplomacy to get Israel and Egypt to disengage their forces in the Sinai after the 1973 Yom Kippur War.[14] It was also the mode of the Clinton administration's negotiations with North Korea to get Pyongyang to stop building nuclear weapons.[15]

Mediation, Arbitration, Adjudication

When countries are at an impasse in their efforts to negotiate a mutually acceptable outcome to a dispute that threatens to escalate to violence, instead of reverting to threats and counterthreats, they have the option of asking an impartial third party (whether an individual, a panel, or an institution) to provide a judgment of how the dispute should be settled. This approach can provide parties to a conflict with a face-saving means of accepting compromises that they would find politically embarrassing if it looked like they were conceding to the demands of their opponents.

The easiest of the devices to invoke is *mediation* (sometimes called conciliation), in which the parties to the conflict are free to accept or reject the findings and proposals of a mediator. To avoid nuclear war, President John F. Kennedy was prepared to ask U Thant, the secretary-general of the United Nations, to mediate his dispute with Nikita Khrushchev over the Soviet missiles in Cuba if the quid pro quo Kennedy offered the Soviet leader failed to resolve the crisis.

Countries are much more reluctant to submit their disputes to *arbitration* (typically by a specially appointed panel) or *adjudication* (usually by a permanently seated commission or court), for these processes require the parties to agree in advance to accept the findings and/or awards resulting from the process. There are, however, functioning arbitration/adjudication processes in the trade field, in the form of the dispute-resolution panels of the World Trade Organization (WTO), and in the ecological field, in the form of regional fisheries commissions—both of which the United States has accepted. If Washington is to help the world build a transnational accountability system, which I advocate in chapter 10, it will have to be more willing and supportive of the evolution of arbitration and adjudication processes in other fields as well.

International "Peacekeeping"

Unfortunately, in all too many cases, none of the measures discussed previously will be sufficient to prevent conflicts between or within countries or among transstate adversaries from escalating to large-scale violence. And once that happens, it is enormously difficult for outsiders whose primary immediate interest is to stop the killing to intervene with sufficient force to bring about a cease-fire, without themselves becoming drawn into the fray and being regarded by one side or the other (or both) as enemies. But in those situations where active hostilities have receded and the belligerents have disengaged their forces (for whatever reason—external pressure, intrawar mediation, or the temporary exhaustion of the warring parties), there can be sufficient time and physical space to interpose UN or non-UN "peacekeepers" to prevent a resumption of the violence and to help eliminate the conditions that precipitated it. The world can only benefit from an enhancement of such a capacity.

I put the term *peacekeepers* in quotation marks to indicate that the function of any such intervention may or may not be, strictly speaking, to keep in place anything more than a fragile cease-fire or truce and also to recognize that there is disagreement among UN peacekeeping officials and experts as to what distinguishes peacekeeping from peace *enforcement*, peace-*making*, or peace-*building*.[16] From here on, though, I will use the term in its broad generic sense to denote the intraconflict or posttruce deployment of forces—not allied with any of the belligerent parties—whose primary mission is to stanch and/or prevent the resumption of violent hostilities.

One of the problems with attempting to rely on peacekeeping missions to substantially reduce the role of force in world affairs is that, given the persistence of sovereignty-respecting norms, peacekeeping missions are unlikely to be authorized and deployed into any locale without the express consent of the major belligerent adversaries. These norms can be overcome in the extreme cases of genocide or crimes against humanity. And they are under challenge by an alternative set of norms, with a growing number of advocates among influential international legal theorists and statespersons, holding that (1) sovereignty carries with it the responsibility to protect the basic safety and elemental well-being of the people within one's jurisdiction, and (2) where this responsibility is not being exercised, the international community has the right—indeed, the obligation—to take over that responsibility, by force if necessary.[17] Still, even in cases of blatant genocide, as in the Sudan today, neither the United Nations nor its most powerful members have been willing to override the legalistic and political obstacles the involved governments (often themselves aiding the perpetrators of the genocide) keep putting in the way of the deployment of international forces strong enough to stop the interethnic massacres.

Despite the legal and traditional normative inhibitions and despite the practical difficulty of generating sufficiently well-trained and well-equipped contingents from countries willing to have their military or police personnel so employed, the UN has undertaken more than sixty peacekeeping missions since 1945. Enlisting personnel from more than forty-five countries, these missions have been instrumental in disarming hundreds of thousand of belligerents. And as of this writing, despite the polyarchic cross pressures that often frustrate efforts to obtain the required authorizing votes in key UN agencies, there are twenty UN peacekeeping missions in operation, with over 100,000 personnel, costing the UN and its members over $5 billion a year. In addition, there are some 7,500 peacekeeping personnel deployed in various trouble spots by regional (non-UN) organizations, at a total cost to the involved nations of over $400 million.[18]

Unavailable in sufficient strength for many of the conflicts currently jeopardizing peoples' lives and/or regional and international stability (e.g., in Darfur, the Congo, Sri Lanka, and the Israel-Gaza border) and showing at best only partial success where they *have* been deployed, such peacekeeping missions are nonetheless on the side of the overall world interest in reducing the use of violence. Instead of focusing on what the UN, other multilateral agencies, and, where necessary, ad hoc coalitions of the willing have not been able to accomplish, Higher Realism counsels supporting their efforts, including through additional funding, in order to improve their capacity to rapidly deploy conflict-control forces into situations where they have a reasonable prospect of success.

And finally, once the United States is able to reduce the demands on its military personnel resulting from the current deployments in Iraq and Afghanistan, consideration should be given to allowing U.S. citizens to volunteer for service in a standby international peacekeeping force.

CHAPTER FIVE

Alleviating Poverty and Disease

U nlike Conventional Realism, which typically has been indifferent to the destitution of peoples in countries of no tangible
geopolitical or economic significance to the United States,
Higher Realism is concerned about extreme poverty and disease wherever
they occur, for two elementary reasons. First, as contemporary medical
and behavioral sciences reveal, it is extremely difficult to confine disease
and other consequences of poverty to the particular locales where they are
prevalent—due to the natural and highly motivated mobility of human
and nonhuman carriers, the millions of refugees from poverty-stricken
areas, and the diseases transmitted by infected travelers and contaminated
cargoes. And second, because world and national interests increasingly
require global society to act as a human community of mutual accountability and responsibility, it is imperative that the better-off members
of global society demonstrate a genuine concern about the suffering of
their fellow humans and a credible determination to find ways of alleviating it.

I speak of *alleviating*—rather than *eliminating*—poverty and disease because, as guidance for foreign policy, world interests should be

achievable, through practical initiatives that can be currently initiated and periodically assessed and adapted to changing circumstances. If absolute goals that are unachievable in the foreseeable future are put forward as world interests, disillusionment and pessimism, if not cynicism, about how realistic those goals may be will likely result. The urgent world interest in *reducing* poverty and disease, together with the human suffering and societal dislocations they are producing, is too important to be dismissed as utopian.

The Millennium Development Goals

The understanding that alleviating poverty is a world interest that is also in the national interest of their respective countries was affirmed by 189 heads of state at the UN summit meeting in September 2000, and it has been reaffirmed by most of the national governments periodically since then. Using 1990 as a base year and looking ahead to 2015, the Millennium Declaration, approved at the UN summit of 2000, set forth the following so-called Millennium Development Goals (MDGs):

- Halve the proportion of people whose income in less than $1 a day;
- Halve the proportion of people who suffer from hunger;
- Ensure that children everywhere will be able to achieve a full course of primary schooling;
- Eliminate gender inequality in all levels of education;
- Reduce by two-thirds the under-five mortality rate;
- Reduce by three-quarters the maternal mortality rate;
- Halt and reverse the spread of HIV/AIDS;
- Halt and reverse the incidence of malaria and other major diseases;
- Integrate the principles of sustainable development into country policies and programs and reverse the loss of environmental resources;

- Halve the proportion of the population without sustainable access to safe drinking water and basic sanitation;
- Improve the lot of at least 100 million slum dwellers;
- Address the special needs of the least developed countries, land-locked countries, and small-island developing states;
- Develop further an open, rule-based, predictable, and nondiscriminatory trading and financial system;
- Deal comprehensively with developing countries' debts;
- Develop and implement strategies for securing decent and productive work for youth; and
- Make available the benefits of new technologies, especially information and communications technologies.[1]

In evaluating developments in these areas in 2007, halfway to the Declaration's target year for the full attainment of the MDGs (2015), the UN Secretariat found, in the words of Secretary-General Ban Ki-Moon, that "our collective effort is mixed." Although some gains had been made, there was "a clear need for political leaders to take urgent and concerted action, or many millions of people will not realize the basic promises of the MDGs in their lives."[2] Specifically, the 2007 assessment made the observations that follow.

Although the proportion of people living in extreme poverty—on less than $1 a day—had decreased in many regions, in sub-Saharan Africa, despite marginal reductions in some countries, approximately 40 percent of the people were still barely surviving at this far-below-subsistence level. And approximately one-third of all the people on earth lived on under $2 per day—the standard for bare subsistence. Given the meager progress made in this regard, tens of millions of children around the world will continue to go hungry unless the conditions they live in are dramatically corrected.

The under-five mortality rate for children had declined globally; yet in 2005 (the latest year with reliable data), over 10 million died before their fifth birthday. And the pace of progress was uneven across regions and countries. In sub-Saharan Africa, the under-five mortality rate exceeded 150 per 1,000 live births (down from 185 in 1990 but still an alarming indicator of the persisting lack of basic health services). Also, half a million women continued to die each year during pregnancy or childbirth.

The prevalence of HIV had leveled off in the developing world while increasing in the world as a whole (affecting 39.5 million people at the end of 2006, up from 32.9 million in 2001). In the hardest hit areas, more than half of those infected with HIV were women. AIDS deaths were highest in sub-Saharan Africa, surpassing 20 million there annually by the end of 2006 and creating a new social problem: orphans. The MDG report estimated that in 2005, some 15.2 million children had lost one or both of their parents, and it predicted that by 2010, there would be 20 million orphans—again, for the most part, in poor countries unable to provide adequate social services for them.[3]

With roughly half of the growing urban population in the developing regions living in slums, soaring unemployment rates (30 percent of working-age youth are unemployed in northern Africa), and unfulfilled demands for basic social services, the prospects are high for explosive discontent to be mobilized by radical demagogues as well as democratic reformers.

And in many developing countries, fodder is provided for the opposition to the market-oriented reforms insisted on by the World Bank and the International Monetary Fund (IMF) (see the discussion in chapter 6 of the "Washington Consensus"), which have often required the postponement of "social overhead" programs in the service of fiscal discipline. Similarly, there is significant opposition to the stated Millennium Development Goal of developing "an open, rule-based, predictable, nondiscriminatory trading and financial system."

Skeptics, such as New York University economist William Easterly, are saying, "We told you so." Setting out such general goals in the form of quantitative world targets to be achieved, they contend, is the kind of top-down abstract "planning," disconnected from the varied particularities of each local situation, that is bound to fail.[4] The champions of the MDG approach, such as British prime minister Gordon Brown and

Columbia University economist Jeffrey Sachs, argue that implementation strategies must, of course, be flexible and responsive to local needs and cultural contexts and that when efforts fall short of the goals, it is largely because of a lagging mobilization of the required resources.[5] Higher Realism welcomes these debates over *how* to improve the condition of the poorest people around the world, for they reflect the premise, increasingly prominent among economists, statespersons, and the attentive public, that this *is* a world interest that is in the national interest of their respective countries.[6]

Recognizing that hardly any of the Millennium Development Goals could be reached without a substantial transfer of resources to the poor countries, most of the affluent industrialized countries (but not the United States) at the 2002 Monterey Conference on Financing for Development reiterated long-standing commitments to provide at least 0.7 percent of their gross national income for development assistance. Other promises have been made periodically, such as the pledges at the 2005 summit of the Group of 8 industrialized nations in Gleneagles, Scotland, to double aid to Africa by 2010, but tangible implementation is slow. At the time of this writing, the only donors to have achieved the Monterey goal of contributing at least 0.7 percent of the gross national income were Denmark, Luxembourg, the Netherlands, Norway, and Sweden. Consequently, as pointed out in the 2007 Millennium Goals report, "the present rate of increase in core development programs will have to triple over the next four years if donors are to deliver on their promises."

Thus far, the most significant progress toward MDG targets in both fund-raising and program implementation has been achieved by the Global Fund to Fight AIDS, Tuberculosis, and Malaria. As of mid-2007, the Global Fund could point to more than 30 million bed nets distributed, more than 1 million people put on antiretroviral treatment, and 2.8 million people treated for TB.[7]

Disease control is one area of foreign assistance to help the unfortunate in which the United States, during the administration of George W. Bush, has made substantial financial contributions. It is also an arena in which that administration's preferences for working unilaterally (reflected

99

particularly in its unwillingness to fund World Health Organization [WHO] AIDS-related programs that provide access to condoms and other birth-control options) have complicated, if not undermined, important multilateral initiatives in the disease-control field.

The New Food-Supply Crisis

The extent to which poverty around the world is the product of systemic factors beyond the control of the poor countries themselves—and therefore requiring systemwide counteraction—is dramatically evident in the food sector, with its volatile supply, demand, and price fluctuations. The food supply (and price) crisis of 2008, provoking riots from Haiti to Pakistan, is attributable to a set of diverse yet interacting trends: the soaring price of oil, which increases the costs of growing food grains and getting them to market; the conversion of corn and food grains into biofuels; the increasing competition for land by other than grain-producing users; the steeply rising food consumption in high-population-growth countries such as China and India, whose economies are rapidly developing; and finally, severe droughts, such as the ten-year-old drought in Australia, that are probably an early symptom of the global warming phenomenon.[8]

The president of the World Bank, Robert Zoelick, estimates that the gains in economic growth around the world since the mid-1990s are in danger of being wiped out as the current inflation of prices for food push at least 100 million people back into extreme poverty.[9] Ironically, responsibility for the current poor condition of the agricultural sector in many developing countries, especially in sub-Saharan Africa, must be laid at the feet of the World Bank itself and the IMF, which imposed government austerity programs as a condition for countries to qualify for the international assistance. In the words of a comprehensive report by the UN Food and Agriculture Organization, "Government budget cuts made in the wake of structural adjustment programs have affected agriculture more than other sectors."[10]

The political reverberations from development backsliding in the agriculture sector of poor countries can be serious and widespread. As El Salvador's president, Elias Antonio Saca, put it, "How long can we stand this situation? We have to feed our people, and commodities are becoming scarce. This scandalous storm might become a hurricane that could upset not only our economies but also the stability of our countries."[11]

Unless and until fundamental remedies in the global economic system are devised to combat such acute and chronic food shortages, direct help can be provided to poor countries that are also food commodity producers—in the form of assistance in boosting their food production. The delivery of emergency food relief, though needed on purely humanitarian grounds, does nothing for (and in some cases may actually retard) the alleviation of overall global food scarcity. And the concept of providing financial aid to countries that are food producers while also requiring them to purchase food from donor-country producers should be discarded. The poor food-producing countries need, above all, better agricultural technologies from the affluent countries. These technologies and training in their use, plus improved seeds, can be provided directly through bilateral or multilateral arrangements; alternatively, special funding can be provided for acquiring equipment and pursuing projects (for water use, sustainable land management, fertilizing, and so on) designed to increase productivity.[12] This brings us to the issue of the role of foreign aid in pursuing the world and national interest in alleviating poverty and disease.

The Foreign Aid Controversy

Official Development Assistance (ODA)—popularly called foreign aid—to poor countries (mostly in the form of direct monetary grants or loans at below-market rates of interest) faces an uphill battle. Unless a potential recipient is geopolitically significant or economically important (despite its needy condition) to the United States, it continues to be difficult to generate sufficient congressional support for providing these funds, which are often described as "giveaways." Proponents of the altruistic aid must overcome three standard objections: (1) that any such resource transfers—if Americans are to fund them out of the goodness of their hearts—should go, first and foremost, to the domestic needy within the United States; (2) that foreign aid distorts the market, artificially supporting those who are inefficient and creating a kind of "moral hazard" by rewarding their uncompetitiveness—all of which only perpetuates their dependence on aid rather than stimulating their own development; and (3) that foreign aid is "money down the drain," for given the corruption and overbureaucratization in the recipient countries, the funding never really materializes in substantial help to the poor.

The first objection assumes there is an unavoidable and unpalatable trade-off between financing domestic "safety nets" and financing international ones. In an immediate sense, this assumption would appear to be true, if the money comes out of the same pot. But if the sizes and numbers of the pots are increased through imaginative global revenue-raising instruments and facilities, the zero-sum definition of the trade-offs can be supplanted by a positive allocation definition. Such new revenues, earmarked for the provision of global public goods, can be sought from industries, firms, and people active in international commerce, especially users of the international "commons" resources—the oceans, seas, major inland waterways, the atmosphere, and outer space (e.g., the electromagnetic frequency spectrum and the geostationary orbit). Relatively small per-voyage or per-activity user fees would raise enormous sums for allocation to economic development and/or environmental protection projects (as compared with the moneys now contributed through ODA), and these surcharges would barely be felt by individual consumers of the products and services offered by the commons-user firms.[13]

The second standard objection to foreign aid—that it deals only with the poverty symptoms of underdevelopment, not its causes, and that it perpetuates the dependency of the poor on their rich benefactors—should be taken seriously, for it directs our attention to the pitfalls of particular kinds of foreign aid. The numerous stories of misbegotten programs, grist for the mill of those who disparage aid, should not, however, be allowed to obscure the need and value of resource transfers that are well thought out. Nor should the moral hazard of outright doles to supplicants be extrapolated to denigrate the kind of foreign aid that is directed toward the stimulation and improvement of productive capabilities and ultimately self-sustaining economic development in the recipient countries. And the fear of fostering fiscal irresponsibility via soft loans to inefficient social democratic–style governments should not mean that external support should go only to structural change (privatization) and basic economic infrastructure investment while deferring all external help for social welfare and human capital development. Even William Easterly, a trenchant critic of the failures in existing aid programs, has granted the importance of "giving the poorest people the health, nutrition, education, and other inputs that raise the payoff of their own efforts to better their lives."[14]

The third objection to providing foreign aid for the poor is that even when extended with good intentions and on the basis of reasonably accurate knowledge of the economic situation in the target locale, much of the assistance (whether money, goods, or technologies) never gets to those most in need in all too many cases. This happens because of the overbureaucratization of the aid-delivery process at both the donor and receiver ends as well as the prevalence of corruption at many points in the distribution chain for funds, contracts, and even foods and medicines. Horror stories such as aid funds being pocketed by military dictators or food rotting on the docks are commonplace. But the answer should not be to cut off the aid and leave even more babies to die of malnutrition. Rather, procedures need to be developed to ensure transparency and accountability up and down the disbursement-delivery chain—which is more the province of experts in public administration rather than economists. An important means for improving transparency and accountability is for the development assistance to be extended to projects that can be monitored during their implementation, as distinct from funding entire government-run programs. Indeed, the World Bank has increasingly adopted this mode of extending loans—at times over the objections of recipient governments that dislike the intrusions into their sovereignty. It should be expected that developing countries seeking loans will be even more uncomfortable if the project monitoring is done by the United States rather than a multilateral agency, but transparency and accountability should be insisted on as a legitimate quid pro quo for the provision of any U.S. aid. Insofar as the resource transfers get diverted or stolen or fall far short of accomplishing their purposes, it is not an inherent fault of foreign aid per se, as some critics claim, but rather a potentially correctable problem resulting from how particular programs and projects are organized.

The Larger Picture

Depending on how it is viewed, the world's glass for measuring the alleviation of poverty and disease cannot yet be characterized as even half full. But since the turn of the millennium (prior to the food-supply crisis of 2008), the one-third-full mark has, roughly speaking, been reached—in other words, we still have two-thirds of the way to go to achieve the Millennium Development Goals. The most sluggish region is sub-Saharan Africa, where there has been starkly uneven growth but also a disturbing downturn in some areas. Yet data gathered by development experts in the UN Secretariat show that:

- The proportion of humans living in extreme poverty has fallen from nearly a third to less than a fifth. The absolute numbers have not declined due to population growth but have leveled off, even in sub-Saharan Africa.
- Child mortality has declined globally—largely due to the work of international programs for controlling malaria and tuberculosis. The African success stories have come from Niger, Togo, Zambia, and Zanzibar.
- Access to uncontaminated water and sanitation has increased, notably in Senegal and Uganda. But looming water shortages in

dry areas of the African continent due to global warming and desertification may reverse this trend.

- There has been progress in getting more children into school in the developing world; about 90 percent are now enrolled in primary schools. Impressive results in Africa have been registered in Ghana, Kenya, and Tanzania.

- Women's political participation—widely recognized as both a reflection and a driver of socioeconomic development—has been growing. The progress has been slow in predominantly Muslim countries, but it is evident even there.[15]

The larger global picture, however, despite the progress, is one of very uneven growth and in some regions and within some countries—middle- and high-income countries included—a widening gap between the affluent and the poor.[16] It is not simply the tangible and absolute economic conditions of the poorer segments of society that are a source of political alienation and radicalism. The resentments, easily whipped up by demagogic politicians, are equally the product of perceptions of *relative* deprivation, even on the part of those whose condition has improved somewhat but who resent the comparative opulence of the wealthy. And these resentments translate into attacks on globalization—the spread of the free-market economy around the world—which is alleged in many quarters to be a principal cause of the perceived growing inequalities.

Thus, the world interest in alleviating poverty and disease—warranted on grounds of the direct impact on the lives of one-fifth of humanity and the impossibility of quarantining the effects of failure—connects to the world and vital U.S. national interest in the norms and forms of the global economic system itself, the subject of the next chapter.

Maintaining a Well-Functioning
Global Economy

The unavoidable fact of life that people everywhere, whether they like it or not, are affected by what happens in the global market for exchanging goods, services, and capital means that there is a world interest in how that market functions, and there is certainly a U.S. interest in its functioning well. Although there is considerable controversy among countries and within the United States itself over the components of a well-functioning global economy, there are a few desiderata that are self-evidently in the interest of all, namely: that exchanges of goods, services, and capital are peaceful and noncoerced; that all those who want to participate are permitted to do so as long as they abide by the basic rules; that the rights to buy and sell are nondiscriminatory, in that *all* who participate are able to freely seek out and purchase for the lowest prices offered and *all* are able to freely sell at the highest prices at which there are buyers; and that the worth of participants' promissory notes (currency, money) for deferring exchanges are reasonably stable and predictable—that is, not subject to such wild fluctuations in their exchange value that trading breaks down.

Higher Realism recognizes and endorses globalization—the basic trend toward an economically integrated world market of largely free trade and investments—regarding it as the natural and ultimately unavoidable result of the technological triumph of mobility of things and information over efforts to prevent their circulation. But Higher Realism also recognizes that progress toward the global free market will, along the way, benefit certain countries and communities more than others, threatening the well-being and survival of those that are ill equipped to compete effectively in the evolving world economy. It may well be that, as the saying goes, a rising tide lifts all boats, but some that are insufficiently seaworthy may capsize. Indeed, in every country, there will be a substantial number of losers as well as winners, not only in the economic game per se but also in the political arena (due to the redistributions of power and authority produced by success or failure in the economy) and indirectly in the cultural sphere (as traditional ways of life are assaulted by more marketable ones).

Here, I am not talking mainly of the severely deprived peoples that are the concern or subject of the Millennium Development imperatives discussed in chapter 5. Rather, I refer to those countries and communities that, because of their actual or perceived *relative* uncompetitiveness in the emerging global system, are opposed to the evolving structure and free-market norms—even those that could benefit them over the long run. John Maynard Keynes's ironic quip that "in the long run we'll all be dead" is appropriate to recall, for it reminds us that politics, which thrives on short-run discontent, will often disrupt basically valid policy based on abstract rational theory unless such policy also addresses and attempts to ameliorate its negative side effects.

The "Washington Consensus" Revisited

In the 1980s, the consensus among leading economists in the International Monetary Fund, the World Bank, and the U.S. Treasury Department about how countries—especially developing countries and former members of the Soviet bloc—should manage their economies established, for a time, key parameters for the management of the globalizing economy as a whole. These parameters were fiscal discipline, meaning that governments should not incur major budgetary deficits; privatization of state enterprises; and market liberalization, including opening up one's economy to free international trade. A country's access to funds for assisting its development was to depend on its adherence to conditions laid down by the lenders for implementing these policies.

But this so-called Washington Consensus has been coming under increasing challenge. Joseph E. Stiglitz, former senior vice president of the World Bank, explains why. According to his analysis, the move to push governments out of the business of providing public services—the government enterprises being inefficient and a cause of budget deficits—was based on overconfidence that competitive free markets would arise quickly to meet the peoples' needs. Moreover, privatization, especially when this meant turning the function over to an unregulated monopoly, often resulted in both price rises for consumers and a dismissal of unproductive government workers "with no sensitivity to social costs." Stiglitz affirms that privatization is often an effective way to restructure a country's economy. But he warns against assuming that the benefits will be automatic or well distributed within the society. And (looking especially at Russia), he identifies the problem of systemic corruption in turning state enterprises over to officials or their friends with an inside track.[1]

Even the trade liberalization centerpiece of the Washington Consensus warrants a second look. Coming from a Nobel Prize–winning economist and one of the formulators of the Washington Consensus—not a populist politician—the following critique from Stiglitz must be taken seriously when developing policies for a the global economy:

Trade liberalization is supposed to enhance a country's income by forcing resources to move from less productive uses to more productive uses: as economists would say, utilizing comparative advantage.... IMF ideology holds that new, more productive jobs will be created as the old, inefficient jobs that have been created behind protectionist walls are eliminated. But that is simply not the case.... The IMF in many countries has made matters worse, because its austerity programs also entailed such high interest rates ... that job and enterprise creation would have been an impossibility.... The necessary capital for growth is simply too costly.[2]

Stiglitz points out that where impressive economic growth and job creation has taken place in developing countries—notably in East Asia—trade liberalization was instituted gradually and in a sequenced way that gave priority to export expansion. Like the United States in its early developmental history, these countries reduced their protective barriers systematically, gradually phasing them out when new jobs were created.

The growth of populist/nationalist political reactions to free trade where promises of development fail to materialize is understandable—especially where conditions appear to be getting worse. But this should not lead to a retraction of existing trade liberalization pacts or a retreat from efforts to negotiate additional agreements, for the basic prescription of expanding wealth by enlarging markets remains sound. To further the world and U.S. interest in a well-functioning global economy, greater attention needs to be given to the worldwide provision of safety nets for countries and communities that are experiencing the destabilizing consequences of uneven development. I will elaborate on safety nets and other ameliorants for uneven development later in this chapter.

Reregulating Capital Markets?

Another culprit, expressing the philosophy of the Washington Consensus, has been the extension of the deregulation frenzy, emanating largely from the United States in recent decades, to capital markets. Under considerable prodding from U.S. financial experts and the IMF, developing countries reduced their controls on money moving in and out of their banks in order to attract investments. But this also attracted speculative money—most of it being gambled on quick profits from exchange-rate fluctuations. Too many poor-risk loans were made with assets originating abroad, so when recipients began to default, the consequent local and regional financial crises (as in the 1997–1998 "Asian crisis") quickly escalated to global proportions.

The motivation of international bankers to provide, through deregulation, more liquidity for economic expansion in the developing world is laudable. But the lesson of the late 1990s crises is that, if anything, smarter and more globally extensive banking regulation—involving enhanced transparency and accountability—is required. The challenge is to accomplish the needed regulation without thereby inhibiting entrepreneurs in developing countries from taking the risks needed for their nations to prosper. Constructively dealing with this dilemma necessitates a continuing open and intensive global dialogue in which the world interest in overcoming the politically destabilizing effects of uneven development is a paramount focus.

Those who are involved in the dialogue and concerned with deriving lessons for policy should take account of the fact that one of the countries that best weathered the past crisis and its economically constricting effects—Malaysia—had been operating with banking regulations that substantially exceed what most Western economists had regarded as sufficient. And then, of course, there is China, which—while liberalizing its economy and still maintaining a high degree of state participation in and control of the market—was able to proceed with its upwardly booming development despite the international economic downturn. Here, I do not mean to imply that heavier state regulation of banking should be considered a prescription for everyone (although it might seem attractive in the wake of the spreading effects of the subprime mortgage crisis of 2008); rather, I would suggest that a more pluralistic approach, granting and learning from different money cultures (and not insisting on a worldwide banking monoculture), ought to be encouraged.

CHAPTER SIX

Avoiding Politically Destabilizing Economic Inequalities

A degree of inequality can be regarded as an indication that the global market is operating as it should, since free competition is supposed to produce winners and losers. Indeed, the inequalities can be seen as a symptom of the essential health of the system and its capacity to reward innovations that make for efficiency and benefits, in the form of reduced prices to consumers and the willingness of entrepreneurs to invest in new product lines.

But when the inequalities produce resentments in parts of society in terms of their relative deprivation—especially when the relative deprivation or, worse yet, the absolute decline in economic well-being can be attributed to avoidable or correctable public policies—the scene is set for domestic political upheaval. Moreover, when the alleged culprit of the resented inequalities is either the free-trade regime itself or foreign investors, such domestic upheaval can translate into protectionist policies that undermine the functioning of the global economy and destabilize international politics.

We must, therefore, question whether the inequalities that people are protesting are avoidable or correctable. And to the extent that they are, Higher Realism—which is concerned with the political effects and not just the economic effects—requires that statespersons search for both prophylactic and remedial correctives. But the choice of corrective policies must also be constrained by assessments of whether they are likely to have deleterious effects on the world economy that ultimately will produce even wider discontent and deeper destabilization.

Causes of the Problematical Inequalities

One of the principal targets of the antiglobalization protests, the International Monetary Fund, itself identified three developments that can be regarded as plausible causes of the inequalities that are making people angry: trade liberalization, financial globalization, and technological progress. The differential impacts of the processes that the IMF staff economists have found to be affecting inequality are summarized in the pages that follow.[3]

Trade Liberalization

Contrary to popular notions that the North American Free Trade Agreement (NAFTA) and other free-trade agreements have exacerbated inequalities between and within countries, the net effects of tariff reductions on trade have been positive in terms of reducing income inequality. This has been particularly noticeable for countries whose foreign earnings come mostly from agricultural exports and especially in developing countries where agriculture still employs a large share of the workforce. Also, for advanced economies, the processed or manufactured imports from developing countries, usually selling at lower prices than domestically produced goods, actually raise the "effective income" of poorer segments of the population because such goods account for a greater share of their consumption as compared to that of the richer segments. The widely held assumption that the importation of such lower-priced goods is the source of greater unemployment in the advanced economies and therefore of greater income inequality is not borne out by the aggregate data. Rather, the overall impact is usually in the direction of *reduced* income inequality. This is because when the lower-priced imports cause the local production of such goods to shut down, the response is often job substitution, as workers in the lower-paying low-end manufacturing sector take jobs in the higher-paying service sector (for example, retail positions).[4]

The cumulative *positive* results of trade liberalization do not, of course, wipe away the temporary economic suffering and psychological despair of those who have lost their jobs (often their medical insurance and other benefits as well) and are forced to compete for new jobs requiring different aptitudes and skills. Moreover, although they are a minority of the labor force, such temporarily displaced workers, together with their families, can constitute a potent anti–free trade political force when mobilized as voting constituents of members of Congress or aspirants to the presidency.

Financial Globalization—Especially Foreign Direct Investment

Inequality within countries does appear to be exacerbated by the global proliferation of foreign direct investment (FDI)—the agents of which are often multinational corporations. In addition to transferring financial capital into the recipient countries, as the large globally active banks do,[5] the manufacturing sector multinationals also transfer technologies and skills that can positively contribute to a country's overall economic development and export diversification—thus, their increasing popularity with developing country governments. Yet according to one theory reflected in the IMF report, because FDI tends to take place in more skill-intensive and technologically intensive sectors, which increases the demand for relatively skilled workers in host developing countries and depletes the demand for relatively *un*skilled workers in the advanced world, the effects of both the inward-moving and the outward-moving FDI widen the income gaps in both poor and affluent countries. This explanation is consistent with the complaint of unionized workers in the manufacturing sector in the United States who have become unemployed due to shutdowns of local factories, that is, that the multinationals are exporting their jobs to lower-wage countries with weak or nonexistent unions. Looking at the country as a whole, it can be expected that even though the inequality impact will dissipate over time as the workers acquire the education and skills needed in other sectors, the anger of the laid-off workers in the politically relevant short run may lead to legislation that will penalize those firms that are moving their factories to countries with lower input costs.

Technological Progress

Income inequality in both advanced and developing economies is most strongly driven by technological progress, which places a premium on the technical skills and literacy that are usually acquired by those who have the time and income to obtain them.[6] In the advanced economies, the demand for higher skills is widespread in manufacturing industries as well as services. Furthermore, even in low-skill manufacturing processes, the increasing use of automation is displacing human labor. In the words of the IMF economists who authored the *Globalization and Inequality* report, "Across the whole sample of countries, technological progress is seen to be the main driver of the fall in the income share of the bottom quintile [of the population] and the rise of the income share of the top quintile."[7]

Rising Demand for Oil

Unless the demand for oil levels off and then drops off—which is highly improbable in the near term although plausible in the longer term if alternative sources of energy are developed—the middle and lower classes in all countries will suffer more than the wealthy. The rises in the price of oil that is directly consumed (in vehicles, heating and cooling, and manufacturing) combined with the rises in the price of commodities with oil inputs (particularly food, reflecting the increased costs of its production, transportation to market, and refrigeration) fall especially hard on the poor and lower-middle classes, absorbing a large portion of their income. The prospects that the growing demand for oil will push price inflation higher and higher are driven especially by the dramatic and accelerating industrialization of China and India (each with over a billion people and still growing)—independent of any conflict-related supply interruptions in the Middle East/Persian Gulf area. Efforts to decrease the demand for petroleum in the United States and to shift to consumption of less environmentally injurious energy products, by levying higher taxes on the consumption of gasoline and other petroleum products, will also squeeze the incomes of the lower classes. Meanwhile, strategically motivated efforts to make the United States less dependent on Middle East/Persian Gulf oil are likely to both pinch the poor with continually high or rising oil prices and promote further global warming.

Remedies for the Inequalities

The reports of widening inequalities even as world output increases are not encouraging. Nonetheless, the very fact that the phenomenon is widely reported on—with concern for its destabilizing implications—by established proglobalization agencies such as the International Monetary Fund is a positive indication that the world interest in remedying the inequalities is gaining recognition.

The analysis reflected in these pages, particularly the assertions that expanding free trade is not the culprit and that the proliferation and globalization of FDI and technological progress are, symbiotically, the principal drivers of the persisting (and in some areas growing) inequalities, points to policy responses that need to be explored.

Efforts to restrict foreign direct investment and technological change would be futile in the face of the essentially unstoppable worldwide circulation of information and capital. Weak and vulnerable states, fearful of falling even further behind, may attempt to erect barriers against penetration by the globalizers, and those in advanced states whose jobs have vanished as a result of the volatile relocation of manufacturing firms may demand tax legislation and other disincentives to discourage the international mobility of capital. But such measures are more likely than not to perpetuate and even worsen the competitive disadvantages of the weaker states and economic sectors.

In the realm of finance, the policy reforms that are implied by the preceding analysis should be directed toward broadening access to credit so that the poorer segments of society will have a better chance to partake of the variegated opportunities for participating in entrepreneurial activities. It would be a tragedy if the subprime lending fiasco of the 2007–2008 period were to be taken out on the poor, who were the victims, not the perpetrators, of irresponsible loan practices. The success stories in the field of microcredit, particularly in poor agricultural regions, need to be mined for guidance.

With respect to technological progress, which the majority of economists have come to regard as the principal driver of unemployment, skewed employment opportunities, and other symptoms and reinforcers of inequality, the principal corrective is to make increased education and skill training a high priority—as a global public good. The reason for raising the resources necessary to ensure that the boats of the currently uncompetitive are not engulfed and capsized by the rising tides of globalization is not simply altruistic: it is more than a Good Samaritan impulse to rescue those who are drowning. Rather, it is also—and predominantly—a desire to prevent the growth of an alienated and uncooperative global population of millions or even billions who can destabilize and obstruct the markets and commerce on which we all depend.

CHAPTER SEVEN

Arresting Disturbances
to Vital Ecologies

A long with the mounting evidence that global warming threatens the well-being of people around the world, there is evidence that many less obviously universal environmental threats are severe enough to establish a compelling world interest in countering them. As with the pockets of poverty and disease around the world, many of the ecological impacts of these environmental threats spread far and wide, carried by currents of water and air and by mobile wildlife and organisms, and the economic and political consequences ultimately threaten world peace and security.[1] The UN Environmental Program (UNEP), in its latest *Global Environmental Outlook*, published in October 2007, identified the most serious of these ecological perturbations, all of which are either human induced or, if naturally occurring, not being subjected to the kind of human counteraction that they should be.[2] Specifically:

• Contaminated water, caused by the release of manufacturing, mining, and energy production by-products and sewage into streams, rivers, lakes, inland seas, and the oceans, is the greatest cause of human sickness and death around the world, as well as a major threat to aquatic life. At the same time, excessive withdrawals of surface water and groundwater—in response to drought conditions, because of bad agricultural and land-use practices, and because of industrial use—will subject about 1.8 billion people to conditions of absolute water scarcity by 2025. And two-thirds of all the people in the world could be subject to what the UNEP characterizes as "water stress" unless corrective action is taken. Land degradation and erosion, which is depleting soils of their nutrients, and the shortages and contamination of water are responsible for much of the poverty and many of the diseases that are debilitating a third of the planet's population.

 • Living resources of the oceans, essential as food for many communities, are being subjected to abuse and extinction due to petroleum extraction and transport, mineral mining operations, and our reliance on the oceans as the ultimate receptacles for industrial and human waste. Coastal human habitats and recreational areas are also adversely affected. Moreover, overfishing, abetted by new technologies permitting long-distance harvesting and at-sea processing in factory ships, is endangering the survival of growing numbers of aquatic species. International monitoring agencies report a steady decline in the sustainability of the world's fisheries, down to an alarming 22 percent in 2007 from 40 percent in 1975.[3]

 • Deforestation, in addition to being a major source of the worsening greenhouse effect (because of the resulting decline in CO_2-absorbing foliage), is also a cause of important biodiversity loss. The felling of prime forests, though significantly controlled in temperate areas in recent years due to pressures brought by environmental groups, continues apace in many tropical countries that are dependent on export earnings from the lumber. From 1990 to 2005, people across the world cut down 3 percent of its forests. The resulting biodiversity loss, exacerbated by other assaults on terrestrial and aquatic ecosystems, is more rapid than at any time in human history.[4] According to the UNEP's 2005 Millennium Ecosystem Assessment report, *Ecosystems and Human Well-Being*, 23 percent of all the world's mammals, 32 percent of amphibians, 12 percent of birds, and 25 percent of conifers are threatened with extinction.[5] The alarming disappearance of species has potentially drastic implications for soil formation, nutrient recycling, and pollination and also for medical research crucial to the battle against cancer and other killer diseases.

• Severe air pollution, caused by the effluents of various industrial processes, motor vehicles, energy-generating facilities, and wildfires, is responsible for the premature death of over 2 million people each year. Also, in poor communities, dangerous air pollution characteristically results when biomass and coal are used for cooking and heating.

The ubiquity and abundance of breathable, nontoxic air used to be taken for granted, even where belching industrial smokestacks defined the skyline. The fast-moving atmosphere, it was thought, would dissipate and dissolve any dangerous emissions. When this proved not to be the case, the first response of industrial communities was to raise the heights of their factory smokestacks so that the pollutants would be more effectively dispersed in the atmosphere, but this only exacerbated the pollution suffered in communities downwind.

In communities hundreds of miles removed from the sources of toxic pollution, meteorological and medical studies have traced the etiology of much respiratory illness to industrial effluents that the atmosphere absorbs like a sponge and later drops in the form of toxic substances—"acid" rain or snow—in neighboring territory. Complaints and pressures from downwind communities and countries have resulted in a number of treaties committing the exporters of the air pollutants to modify their culprit industrial processes. The Convention on Long-Range Transboundary Air Pollution, signed by thirty-five countries in 1979, with more members joining the regime in subsequent years, has contributed to a significant yet uneven abatement of the problem in Europe and North America (north of the Rio Grande).

One vulnerable ecological asset that has received impressive ameliorative attention from the nations that were once its principal assailants is the stratospheric ozone layer that shields the Earth from excessive ultraviolet radiation coming from the Sun. If not for this protective envelope, most plants and animals would suffer serious harm from the Sun's rays, including skin cancer for humans. The drastic thinning of portions of the ozone layer observed by meteorologists in the 1970s and the discovery that the major culprit was the chlorine released into the stratosphere by chlorofluorocarbons (CFCs)—the chemical widely used as a coolant in air conditioners and refrigerators and a propellant for aerosol sprays—led environmental interest groups in the United States to sponsor legislation banning processes that involved CFCs. The affected industries and companies, most prominently DuPont, at first lobbied intensely against such prohibitions. But DuPont soon realized it could no longer escape the domestic ban, and it was now concerned about the lack of a level playing field vis-à-vis its international competitors. Consequently, DuPont took the lead in promoting a global phase-out of CFCs and other offending chemicals. The result was the 1987 Montreal Protocol on Substances That Deplete the Ozone and a succession of addenda and implementing meetings over the years. The 2006 meeting of the parties, for example, dealt mainly with exemptions and/or help for developing countries that claimed economic hardship in restricting their chemical uses.[6]

Beyond the stratosphere, the planet's outer space environment, seemingly an endless realm with enough room for all, is also more and more subject to conflict-producing congestion and dangerous uses. Apart from the issue of the militarization of outer space, controversy surrounds the use of a scarce resource: the geostationary orbit, the band of space 22,300 miles above the equator. A satellite deployed in this orbit, inertially traveling at the same speed as the Earth rotates, can see or broadcast to one-third of the globe from its vantage point. This permits coverage of the whole planet by as few as three satellites, whereas at lower orbits, global coverage requires the deployment of many satellites. Moreover, some parts of the geostationary orbit—those over landmasses serviced most heavily—are more valuable than others. As a growing number of countries and corporations come to rely on this outer space resource, congestion and competition for preferred slots of the orbit mount, and those who were slow to enter the space age are unwilling to accept a preemption of the best orbital locations by satellites deployed earlier by the advanced space powers.[7]

Another serious problem in the outer space environment is the debris orbiting the Earth. Old rocket launchers, solar panels, parts of exploded or decaying satellites, and even accidentally dropped tools and photo equipment are endangering the safety of spacecraft and astronauts. The National Aeronautics and Space Administration counted over 9,000 pieces of such space "junk" in early 2008—most of them in low orbit a few hundred miles above the Earth. Both the United States and China contributed to the problem in 2007 and 2008 by shooting down their own spacecraft—China taking out one of its weather satellites and the United States destroying one of its spy satellites. In addition, more than 200 dead satellites are floating in the coveted geostationary orbit, and predictions indicate there will be over 1,000 out there before 2020. The International Association for the Advancement of Space Safety has been warning that a tragedy is in the offing unless the space powers find a way of cooperating to clean up and control the debris.[8]

The Planetary Commons

As with global warming, the intensity and consequences of these ecological disturbances vary between regions and localities, as do the capacities of communities to adapt to or counteract their negative effects. But whether floating in outer space, carried on currents of air and water, or transported via migrations of birds and fish and insects and microorganisms, the ecological perturbations traverse political borders and jurisdictions, and they are often unpredictable—and uncontrollable on a local or national basis. Birds, whales, and fish know what humans have only recently begun to comprehend: that the world as a whole (including its outer space environment) is a vast ecological commons. As put by the UN-appointed Commission on Environment and Development, "The Earth is one but the [political] world is not. We all depend on one biosphere for sustaining our lives. Yet each community, each country, strives for survival and prosperity with little regard for its impact on others.... National boundaries have become so porous that traditional distinctions between matters of local, national, and international significance have become blurred. Ecosystems do not respect national boundaries."[9]

The old British term for cattle-grazing areas open to the herds of all the surrounding villagers was *the commons*, and that word is now often applied to public parks in the centers of New England cities and towns. Using that term in describing the Earth and its atmosphere plus the planet's extra-atmospheric environment provides a useful perspective for designing regimes to deal with the threats to vital ecologies.[10]

The ecological—and political—viability of any resource-commons regime is a function of the abundance or scarcity of the resources the commons provides; whether the valued resources are stationary or mobile within the commons; the interdependence of the resources (with one another inside the commons and with conditions outside the commons); and the physical divisibility of the resources.[11] Where the commons resources are mobile, very difficult to divide, and abundant (meaning not vulnerable to depletion or abuse), a regime of open access and free use makes sense. These conditions were once thought to prevail in the vast ocean waters beyond immediate national coastal limits, in the atmosphere that brings the weather, and certainly in outer space.

The resources in the nonland environments are still highly mobile and largely indivisible. Technological advances have made these realms more accessible, and attempts have been made to extend and delineate national jurisdictions by drawing lines outward from the coasts or upward into the atmosphere and outer space. Yet neither the fish nor the storm clouds nor the planets can be constrained in their movements by such legal/political boundary markers. Nor, with certain exceptions, does it make sense to physically divide up the mobile resources among the nations.

But the other essential condition for sustaining a regime of open access and free use of a commons—that its valued resources are abundant and not subject to depletion through normal use—no longer prevails in Earth's nonland realms. Left to their own devices and market-based decisions, the users (and abusers) of ocean resources (to cite a prime example) are getting in one another's way not only more often but more intensely. But the global public good of ecologically healthy oceans will

not be attained or even rationally pursued without a commons management regime that has the authority to allocate ocean-use privileges
and responsibilities in the world interest. Precedents and rudimentary
institutional scaffolding for the heavier controls that are needed have
been established by the dispute-resolution provisions in the Law of the
Sea Treaty (which, at this writing, the United States still needs to ratify)
and by the capacity of the various international regional fishing commissions to issue seasonal fishing quotas, net size specifications, and other
technical rules and regulations to assure maximum sustainable yields.
But a much greater supranational implementation of the world's interest
in healthy ocean ecologies is required.

The health of the planetary ecological commons, as well as the various
local and particular resource commons that make up the whole, can thus
be recognized as a global public good. A basic commitment to care for the
whole Earth's complex ecology as humankind's commons is important as
a motivating orientation, even though regimes for doing so will vary to
match the different parameters and dynamics of particular ecologies.

The persistence of incongruence between vital ecosystems and the
basic structures and normal functioning of world politics is one of the
targets of Higher Realism. Bringing ecology and polity into congruence
requires an adoption of a world interest and global public goods mind-
set by statespersons, other influentials, and the attentive public—the
norm of accepting responsibility for how one's actions (or neglect) will
affect the health of the planet's commons. The fact that the people and
resources in a particular jurisdiction are not immediately or directly
harmed by behavior that is injurious to ecosystems in other jurisdictions
should not exempt the currently well-off jurisdiction from sharing in
the responsibility for ameliorative action. The ultimate transmissibility,
however inadvertent, of ecological harm across and beyond politically
constructed borders is increasingly recognized. And it is not only the
nonterrestrial realms—the deep ocean and outer space, where claims of
territorial sovereignty are patently absurd—that warrant being designated
"the common heritage of [hu]mankind" but also the entire natural world
within and around the planet.

The assumption of this ecological responsibility *for* all *by* all does not mean that the world's most powerful and legally constituted polities—the nation-states—should be stripped of their sovereignty and have the responsibility for the resources within their jurisdictions transferred to global supranational agencies. On the contrary, Higher Realism recognizes that effective servicing of the world interest in a healthy environment requires first and foremost that the existing nation-states assume responsibility for the care of ecologies located within or traversing their jurisdictions (*their* part of the planetary commons). But Higher Realism also recognizes that nationally formulated and managed programs for exercising this responsibility are often insufficient, especially for globally or transnationally extensive ecologies; in such cases, the national responsibility has to be shared with or supplemented by global or regional regimes. Moreover, insofar as living in a healthy environment is considered a human right, nation-states ought to be subject to the same kind of obligations to provide it as they are for the other human rights discussed in the next chapter—that is, when a national government fails to exercise its responsibility for protecting the elemental rights of its citizenry, the larger (regional or global) society can—or, more strongly, *should*—take on that responsibility.

CHAPTER EIGHT

Promoting Democracy
and Human Rights

I n some quarters, democracy promotion has acquired a bad name due
to its prominence in the worldview of neoconservatives in the Bush
administration as well as the way in which it has been mismanaged
in Operation Iraqi Freedom. But this should not detract from the importance of democracy and human rights as global public goods. The
conviction that governments are illegitimate unless based on the uncoerced consent of the governed stands on its own as an almost universally
embraced moral imperative. Higher Realism takes this into account.

Higher realism also recognizes that the promotion of democracy and
human rights has become a pragmatically justifiable world interest. The
information revolution and the inability of governments to hide their
repressive policies have created situations that are explosive and disruptive
of world order, situations in which consent-of-the-governed principles
and basic human rights are blatantly violated. Attempts by governments
to suppress groups espousing the democratic ethos are likely to stimulate revolts against these very regimes. And such revolts, if they provoke

further (especially violent) repression, make it difficult for prodemocracy governments and political movements to stand idly by without intervening to oppose the brutality. The situation is similar with uprisings against regimes that are systematically suppressing other basic human rights in the international covenants that most countries have ratified: the repression of such uprisings may well provoke violent acts against the regime, including terrorism, and a vicious spiraling of the violence. Again, countries or communities that have taken up the cause of the militant human rights rebels are likely to be motivated to intervene.

Even when the suppression of prodemocracy or human rights uprisings is temporarily successful, the festering of intense and enduring hostility to the regime in power can produce combustible situations that can eventually explode and catalyze full-blown wars. Or, where the repression is decisive and the aggrieved communities see no chance of remobilizing their efforts for a future uprising, the desperate individuals may become homeless refugees, adding to the world's burden of poverty and disease.

Implementation Strategies

Although almost all governments affirm commitments to democracy and human rights (albeit often disagreeing over the definitions), there is a persisting controversy—within and among governments—over implementation strategies. Under what circumstances should democracy and human rights be sacrificed to other world interests? What priorities and sequencing of democratization and the various human rights are justifiable and pragmatically warranted? And what kinds of outside intervention are appropriate to promote democracy and human rights in countries where they are seriously lagging?

Alternative policy approaches in this field operate on the premise that there can often be at least temporary tensions between the material world and national interests, on the one hand, and the norms and forms of good governance, on the other—especially when the governance respects democratization and human rights. The policies reflecting these tensions range from the Conventional Realist approach (subordinating democracy and human rights promotion to economic and standard security interests—the policy of "constructive engagement") to intrusive humanitarianism (insisting on specified significant democratization and human rights improvements in a target country as conditions for obtaining financial assistance and/or a participatory role in international agencies) to military action aimed at deposing the human rights–violating regime. Higher Realism, as will be explained, is neither as indifferent to the domestic political conditions in other countries as is Conventional Realism nor as aggressively insistent on reform as are the humanitarian interventionists.

Constructive Engagement

The prime example of the constructive engagement policy has been the U.S. relationship with China, pursued under successive administrations starting with Richard Nixon's and continuing through George W. Bush's. It received its most thorough high-level review and endorsement under President Bill Clinton. ·

Having campaigned against the reluctance of the previous Bush administration to take a tough stand on China's poor human rights record (epitomized by the violent crackdown on the prodemocracy demonstrators in Tiananmen Square in 1989), President Clinton procrastinated when it came to implementing his promise to deny China normal trading privileges unless Beijing instituted significant human rights reforms. After a multiyear review process, the administration concluded in 1997 that the denial of a normal trading relationship with the United States would not be in the national interest or in the interest of world peace. In the words of Secretary of State Madeleine Albright,

> If the United States, the world's largest and most open economy, were to deny China's normal trading relationship, China's stake in the international system would shrink. The consequences would be grave indeed.

First, ... we could lose China's cooperation on dismantling North Korea's nuclear program.

Second, ... it would disrupt our initiatives to curtail China's transfers of advanced weaponry to unstable regions.

Third, we would risk losing Chinese support for U.S. initiatives at the UN—including ... peacekeeping and sanctions on Iraq. And China, destined to displace the United States as the largest producer of greenhouse gases, could withhold its participation in a global agreement on preventing climate change....

Fourth, [it] ... would devastate our economic relationship. It would invite Chinese retaliation against our exports ... [and] would also damage future opportunities for American investment, as China would steer contracts to our many economic competitors....

Fifth, the damage to our commercial ties could well spill over into our efforts to improve human rights in China.... Chinese leaders might be even less likely to take the actions we have been encouraging to release political dissidents, to allow international visits to prisoners and to open talks with the Dalai Lama on increasing Tibetan autonomy.[1]

In response to criticisms that the policy amounts to a "see no evil, hear no evil, speak no evil" indifference to Beijing's human rights abuses, defenders of the policy claim that flourishing economic intercourse, official interactions in various fields, cultural and educational exchanges, and technological cooperation will all contribute to the gradual opening up of China's political system and eventually to a fuller enjoyment of human rights by its citizens.

Constructive engagement is most compatible with Conventional Realism's respect for national sovereignty and (in its more extreme variants) the corollary proposition that how a government treats its own citizens is nobody else's business. Higher Realism regards constructive engagement as useful in some cases as a fallback strategy—for continuing to deal with regimes that are unsusceptible to pressures for reform of their political processes and human rights abuses, as long as the latter are not so severe as to constitute genocide or other crimes against humanity.

Where there are persisting gross violations of human rights, Higher Realism does not rule out coercive intervention or even military action to force a change in regime.

Spotlighting the Abuses

Not incompatible with constructive engagement, publicly embarrassing governments for denying their citizens basic political and civil rights can, in some cases, induce reform. In a country with a relatively free press and a citizenry that retains the ability to meet and organize peaceful protests, such as Chile in the late 1970s under the dictatorship of Gen. Augusto Pinochet, publicizing the abuses and the denial of democracy (especially if the country is a party to the basic international human rights covenants) can energize the reformers and undercut the claim of the regime in power to be the legitimate caretaker of the nation. This, indeed, is one of the functions of the U.S. State Department's annual *Country Reports on Human Rights*,[2] and that purpose appears to have provided some nontrivial encouragement for the transitions from dictatorship to democracy in Chile as well as in South Korea, Indonesia, and Turkey.

The possible downside to this U.S. strategy of publicly and officially spotlighting countries' human rights abuses around the world is the prospect that in some countries, it will generate a siege mentality on the part of an already vulnerable regime. The regime will then close off, as much as possible, access by its people to such negative reports (e.g., by Internet and e-mail censorship). China, in retaliation for the bad marks it continues to get each year in the State Department's country reports, has taken to publishing its own annual report on human rights abuses in the United States. More important, the United States has to be wary that its seemingly self-righteous accusations about the human rights shortfalls of others do not validate charges of U.S. hypocrisy, given the reports of its own abuses of suspected terrorist detainees in Abu Ghraib and Guantánamo and its transferring of prisoners to countries where they can be subjected to torture.

Conditioning Foreign Aid on Human Rights Performance

If we are serious about democratization and human rights, should we not be willing to go beyond scoring points in the game of vilification and put our money where our mouths are? Just as the agencies involved in fostering economic development have injected macroeconomic policy conditions that aid recipients must fulfill in order to qualify for the assistance, should not the recipients' performance on certain indexes of democratization and human rights also be linked to qualifying for assistance?

The U.S. Congress has answered these questions in the affirmative with respect to "gross violations of internationally recognized human rights," mandating that no economic or military assistance may be provided to the governments of countries the State Department finds are engaged in such violations. In the basic legislation, these gross violations are deemed to include "torture or cruel, inhuman punishment, prolonged detention without charges, [causing] the disappearance of persons, or other flagrant denial of the right to life, liberty, and the security of person ... [such as] internment or imprisonment ... for political purposes."[3]

But in the basic and implementing legislation, the Congress typically permits exemptions from the aid restrictions even for the gross violators if the president determines that an exemption is important for the national interest. Particularly since 9/11, this exemption option has allowed aid packages to be sustained for countries with notorious human rights records provided they are U.S. allies in the war against terrorism. Presidential waivers have also been extended to countries deemed important for controlling the spread of weapons of mass destruction, for de-escalating regional conflicts, and even for the health of the U.S. economy.

So although there is a rather solid consensus that the United States should do what it can to counter gross violations of human rights around the world, when it comes to translating this national conviction into actual policies, the legislation and its interpretation by executive agencies have virtually assured that it will be implemented selectively to serve *other*, more tangible U.S. interests. Conventional Realism tends to support this subordination of human rights to more "vital" U.S. interests. Higher Realism grants that the implementation of the human rights interest should be tailored to the situation at hand and that certain bald coercive strategies, such as cutoffs in economic and military aid, may have to be dropped, deferred, or compromised case by case; it rejects, however, the subordination logic. Rather, Higher Realism argues for an *elevation* of human rights considerations into the counsels of decision—international and domestic—of agencies with economic development and security missions. If trade-offs must be made, their implications for the range of world and national interests must be thoroughly explored; further, it should not be assumed a priori, for example, that a government's cooperation with the United States in counterterrorism operations gives it impunity for brutally suppressing an ethnic self-determination movement.

Defining and Designing Democratization Strategies: The Fallacy of Omniscience

Although human rights and democratization are often lumped together in foreign policy rhetoric—under the rubric of "freedom" or "liberty"—when it comes to designing foreign policies, these sometimes quite different aspects of freedom need to be disaggregated. Democratization issues primarily have to do with the formulation of policy, whereas human rights issues by and large involve the governmental implementation of policy. And whereas it is relatively easy to make the case that there are world and national interests in prohibiting certain kinds of extremely brutal behavior by governments (no matter where they are located, no matter what the culture and history of their peoples), it is more difficult and even wrongheaded to prescribe universally appropriate ways of ensuring that the choice of basic policies within a country will be based on the informed consent of the governed. Nor is there one best pattern for sequencing and phasing in the democratization processes with economic development programs and with efforts to calibrate human rights protections with security and law and order imperatives.

As argued previously, democracy (and therefore democratization) is a worthy world interest. But it is still an experiment in governance that works differently in different economic conditions and cultural settings. Some champions of democracy nevertheless have presumed to generalize about how the system works and how it should be installed all across the world; indeed, this omniscience fallacy has, at times, infected U.S. foreign policy—most notably and perhaps disastrously in Operation Iraqi Freedom.

The official eagerness to induce as many countries as possible to adopt democracy, whatever the difficulties, is, in large part, driven by the notion—supported by numerous social science studies—that democracies rarely, if ever, fight one another.[4] But this "democratic peace" theory, if true (skeptics challenge the definitions and coding of both "democracy" and "peace" that are used in some of the studies), has nothing to say about democratization—the transition to democracy from autocracy—and how that process can be pursued nonviolently.

Political scientists Edward D. Mansfield and Jack Snyder have cogently argued and presented historical data to show that democratization is often violent, characteristically involving challenges to and disruption of existing power relationships and privileges as well as resistance by those who are about to be displaced. And they have called for "humility about the ability of any outsider to reengineer a country's political institutions."[5] Although less pessimistic than Mansfield and Snyder about the prospects for successful democratization, Thomas Carothers, director of the Democracy and Rule of Law Project at the Carnegie Endowment for International Peace, counsels gradualism and a highly adaptive policy that is responsive to the initial lack of a civic culture and supportive institutional structures in many of the target societies; this approach may, however, mean delay in moving toward full-blown electoral competition, which often is, but should not be, equated with democracy.

Warning that dissatisfaction with the social and economic performance of new democratic systems has been growing in the developing world and that there is a reviving attractiveness of the "strong hand" model of development, Carothers advises that "simplistic ... efforts extolling the virtues of democracy are inadequate; more sophisticated efforts that explore the complexities of the issues at stake are needed." Moreover, he wisely cautions that acting as if the United States has a unique calling for democracy promotion sends an unhelpful message to the world and unfortunately prompts a backlash against democracy itself. "If a 'freedom agenda' is to be effective it must not be a U.S. agenda but a global one."[6]

Sequencing Democratization and Economic Development

The constructive engagement approach of postponing demands for democratization in countries controlled by autocrats whom, for economic or geopolitical reasons, the United States does not want to alienate is seen by many development economists as giving license for prioritizing the economic dimensions of development.[7] They argue that even though democratization and economic progress do go hand in hand in many developing countries, it is also true that when democratization precedes or prematurely accompanies the economic policies that can benefit all levels of society, those who are left behind become angry. And as a result, they are easily mobilized by populist demagogues demanding intervention into the market to redistribute wealth and tend to the immediate needs of the poor. In such situations, the constructive engagers (and many development economists) have been willing to turn a blind eye to symbiotic accords that may be formed between the current beneficiaries of the market economy (including U.S. multinational corporations) and the autocrats in power who are fearful of democracy. Some of the contemporary backlashes against democratization in certain Third World countries are a reaction to this symbiotic collusion.

This theory of pursuing economic development first and *then* democratization, together with its policy implications, is challenged in a study by the Council on Foreign Relations. In that study, historical evidence and contemporary assessments of modernization efforts in developing countries are marshaled to show that, more often than not, democratization is either a facilitating precondition or a corollary condition for economic progress. By democratization, however, the authors do not mean simply one person–one vote elections but also the larger panoply of institutions that make for transparent and accountable governance. Accordingly, the aid policies of multilateral institutions (especially the IMF, the World Bank, and regional development banks) and U.S. bilateral assistance programs should be designed to encourage and reward democracy-building and to withhold benefits from recalcitrant regimes (although not in ways that would exacerbate the misery of the helpless poor).[8]

A Prudent U.S. Policy

Given all the uncertainties about the relationships between democratization, human rights, and the overall development of viable nation-states, as well as the contending theories about these relationships, how can we formulate a usable set of guidelines for dealing with adverse political conditions within countries that will not be tarnished by the fallacies of omnipotence and omniscience that have pervaded recent U.S. policies in the developing world?

Early in the administration of Jimmy Carter—the first administration to make democratization and human rights a centerpiece of U.S. foreign policy—Secretary of State Cyrus Vance, facing the inherent uncertainties and dilemmas in attempting to implement this move, formulated such a set of guidelines. Those guidelines merit retrieval for dealing with the paradoxes of the contemporary Polyarchy.

Vance cautioned that "a sure formula for defeat of our goals would be a rigid hubristic attempt to impose our values on others. A doctrinaire plan of action would be as damaging as indifference." We must be realistic, he said: "Our country can only achieve our objectives if we share what we do to the case at hand." This would require applying the following questions to each situation:

"First, what is the nature of the situation in the country of concern?
What kinds of violations or deprivations are there?
Is there a pattern to the violations? If so, is the trend toward concern for human rights or away from it?
What is the degree of control and responsibility of the government involved?
And finally, is the government willing to permit outside intervention?
A second set of questions concerns the prospects for effective action.
Will our action be useful in promoting the overall cause of human rights?
Will it actually improve the specific conditions at hand? Or will it be likely to make things worse instead?
Will the country involved be receptive to our interests and efforts?
Will others work with us, including official and private international organizations dedicated to furthering human rights?
Finally, does our sense of values and decency demand that we speak out or take action anyway, even though there is only a remote chance of making our influence felt?
A third set of questions focuses on the difficult policy dilemmas and tradeoffs.
Have we been sensitive to the genuine security interests, realizing that the outbreak of armed conflict or terrorism could itself pose a serious threat to human rights?
Have we considered all the rights at stake? If, for instance, we reduce aid to a government which violated the political rights of its citizens, do we not risk penalizing the hungry and the poor, who bear no responsibility for the abuses of their government?"[9]

Higher Realism is informed by these complexities. It operates from the premise that the world interest in promoting freedom and democracy is best furthered through such prudential, case-by-case assessments—with substantial input from the locals—of local feasibility and consequences and of expected costs to other world interests rather than on the basis of a universal strategy of democratization. The consideration of appropriate policies, especially when it comes to whether and how to intervene in failed and failing states, is generating intense debate in national and international policy arenas. The very fact of these debates, coupled with their prominence, is symptomatic of the worldwide recognition that the fate of people within countries is not simply the responsibility of the allegedly "sovereign" national governments. Instead, particularly in cases of systemic national failure to protect the people from gross human rights abuses, it is a responsibility we all share.[10]

Higher Realism counsels restraint, however, when it comes to remedying other countries' political and societal shortcomings. How and how fast to democratize, to build up independent judiciaries, to institute due process of law, to remove restrictions on the rights of women, and to protect the rights of religious and cultural minorities are decisions best left to each country. They should be made according to the country's own traditions and/or to the capacity of its reformist citizenry to pressure their government. And where transnational pressures seem needed and likely to strengthen the prospects of human rights groups in particular countries, the best agents for bringing the pressures to bear will probably be nongovernmental organizations (NGOs) with links to the indigenous human reformers rather than other governments. The government-to-government pressures, especially when they take the form of economic sanctions, can be too easily branded by the target government as imperialistic intervention into the country's internal affairs; they can also provide the government with an excuse for persecuting the local reformers as the allies of external enemies.

Political philosopher Michael Walzer has provided a useful formulation for determining which aspects of a country's political way of life should be subject to reformist pressure by foreign governments and which should be left largely to the country to develop and change on its own. The latter, a country's way of life toward which the outside world should be respectfully patient, comprises the "thick," everyday norms of interpersonal relations that have evolved over time and are embodied in a nation's basic political culture and its intricate and deep structure of domestic law. The former, including the prohibitions against genocide, ethnic cleansing, and crimes against humanity, constitutes a "thin" layer of norms and laws governing relations *between peoples of different cultures.*[11] There is a fundamental human interest, as I have argued, in thickening that still-thin layer through an expanding consciousness of world interests. But to confuse an existing thick culture with the thin or to forcibly attempt to impose one's values on the world's thick cultures is not only inconsistent with Higher Realism but also subversive of its spirit. Pursuing a respectful intercultural dialogue and diplomacy is the better course—a topic to which I turn in the next chapter.

Respecting Cultural
and Religious Diversity

H igher Realism operates from the premise that effectiveness in
pursuing each of the world interests requires knowledge of the
diverse cultural settings in which implementing policies will
have to be applied and a willingness to adapt the policies to the norms and
forms that are essential aspects of the diverse cultures. Adaptation does
not mean surrender or total acquiescence to behavior that we find repug-
nant. Nor does it mean refraining from attempts to persuade governments
and groups not to engage in or encourage the offensive behavior. It does
mean that our interactions (even with declared adversaries) should convey
respect for the other's basic culture—unless the intolerable behavior is an
essential part of that culture. In other words, "friendly persuasion" (the
Quaker concept of nonviolent assertiveness) should be the prevailing
ethos for conducting intercultural disputes when the cultural differences
appear to be stumbling blocks to vital cooperation.

This respect for cultural diversity, in addition to being central to the
pursuit of the other world interests, is a value in and of itself. It is in

humankind's interest to have a pluralistic world of nations and communities, each conducting an experiment, as it were, in the best ways for people to live with each other and their fellow creatures on planet Earth. Some of these nations and communities claim to have received (mono) theistic commandments and instructions, others claim polytheistic guidance, and still others induce human behavioral rules from nature's "laws." Finally, there are many within each nation who are skeptical of all-encompassing religions, philosophies, or cosmologies and who are content to let economic and political "markets" determine which behaviors are capable of maximizing well-being.

It has become fashionable in post–Cold War political discourse to dichotomize the world's dominant cultural divides (sometimes called civilizations) into Modern versus Traditional, North versus South, Judeo-Christian versus Islamic, or the grossly inaccurate "West versus the Rest."[1] These oversimplifications are useful to the extent that they remind us before we embark on the next reformist crusade—be it for democratization or human rights or free trade—about the reality of the differing belief systems and ways of life proudly adhered to by billions of people who may not want to emulate our own.

But the dichotomizations are unhelpful and often downright pernicious as guides to actual policy in that they obscure the reality of great and subtle differences *within* each of the polar types of culture or civilization. Thus, the Judeo-Christian category obviously includes an enormous variety of belief systems, some of which differ from each other more than they do from certain of the Islamic theological schools. And the global nation of Islam itself, as many U.S. policymakers have belatedly discovered, comprises (even in the Middle East) members of deeply antagonistic sectarian communities (Shiite, Sunni, Wahhabi) who would rather die than be subjugated to one of the others.

Mindful of such oversimplifications and the pitfalls in trying to translate them into policy, a brief excursion into the differences between so-called Western and non-Western modes of dealing with the various world interests can be useful. In particular, it may prove to be a prophylactic against future hubristic Pax Americana ventures, especially in the "developing" world (another unfortunate categorization, which I still use, that inadvertently implies *they* need major improvement but *we* do not).

Understanding Islam

Inasmuch as 15 percent of the world's inhabitants are Muslims, at least a rudimentary understanding of the Islamic faith—and an awareness of its own pluralistic character—is a requisite of Higher Realism. What Muslims everywhere have in common is a professed adherence to the will of Allah (the one and only true God) as conveyed to the people on Earth by the Prophet Muhammad, the religion's founder.[2] The Prophet's statements of Allah's place in the universe, his power, and his expectations of his human subjects are transcribed in the Koran (or *Quran*) and other reports of what he said and did. Clearly, in today's polyarchic world, the Koran is must reading for the U.S. president and his foreign policy advisers.[3]

But let the buyer beware. The meaning, practical behavior, and legally enforceable implications of the Prophet's words as recorded in the Koran are fervently disputed by his disciples. Thus, the basic law of Islam, or sharia, varies with time and place, and it may well be quite different in Baghdad, Tehran, Istanbul, Islamabad, Dacca, and Jakarta.[4]

That said (and I will elaborate the implications of the pluralistic sharia for Higher Realism shortly), I would point out that most Muslims claim to adhere to at least the following (Koran-prescribed) politically significant tenets:

Allah (God) is the one true sovereign.

In all of Islam, everyone—the ruler and the ruled, the high-born and low-born—is equal in the most important law of life: duty to the will of Allah.

It is the will of Allah that ruler and ruled alike be obligated to serve the well-being of the Islamic *Ummah* (community) as a whole, and ensuring this is the aim of Islamic law on Earth. The Ummah takes precedence over the wants and needs of any individual or family, local community, or official, no matter how high or low in rank.[5]

The traditional interpretation of this emphasis on the oneness of members of the religious community, all submitting to the will of Allah, tended to discourage open dissidence by subjects of an Islamic state against the current governing authorities. If the ruler was acting contrary to the will of Allah, he would be punished in the afterlife, and the pious Muslim who respectfully submitted to the prevailing theocracy's interpretation of the holy law would be rewarded by Allah for his or her piety. But such passive obedience toward regimes in power is no longer the norm in the Islamic world.

Today, when ruler and subject come into conflict and each claims to be acting as Allah and the local sharia tradition prescribe, the issue of *who* on Earth determines what Allah's will entails most often is resolved not on the basis of theology but by who will prevail if the conflict becomes violent. Sometimes, this will be settled by an actual clash of arms or civil war; at other times, cool prewar calculations can avoid the bloodshed. Even the militant jihadists, popularly believed in the West to be eager to martyr themselves in acts of suicidal terrorism against alleged apostates, are hardly all that inclined to sacrifice themselves if they anticipate losing.

The complexities and complications in the pluralistic world of contemporary Islam—which both contributes to and is pervaded by the emergent Polyarchy—should throw a damper on any enthusiasm in Washington for manipulating the political arena in Muslim-dominated jurisdictions, either by divide-and-rule stratagems or by direct military intervention. The United States should also resist the temptation to take sides in secular-versus-Islamic contests for power in the various countries in the Muslim world (Turkey being a case in point) or to favor one group of clerics over another. The scene is often too volatile for even the locals to adequately comprehend and manage, let alone outsiders.

Appreciating "Asian Values"

In various Asian countries—particularly those experiencing relative success in economic growth, cutting across the Cold War division of the region into Communist and non-Communist areas—there is a non-Western philosophical renaissance that needs to be understood and respected. Prominent in Malaysia, Singapore, South Korea, Taiwan, and Hong Kong, it is modernist and procapitalist when it comes to economic development yet rather authoritarian when it comes to political and civil liberty.

This renaissance of traditional Asian values draws support from diverse sources, including the classics of Indian and Chinese philosophy that express the inseparability of individuals and community. This concept stands in contrast to the modern Western notion of perpetual conflict between public and private interests, requiring legalistic and institutional mechanisms to resolve the disputes. The Hindu view, explains former Indian president Sarvepalli Radhakrishnan, holds that "human society is an organized whole, the parts of which are naturally dependent in such a way . . . that the whole is present in each part, while each part is indispensable to the whole."[6]

Similarly, Confucian thought, experiencing a revival in Chinese diaspora communities throughout Asia, maintains that in the "virtuous state," there is no distinction, no separation, and no confrontation between the individual and society but rather an essential unity and harmony, with justice regarded as that which contributes to the harmony.[7] Confucius is quoted as advising the ruler of the state, "If you desire what is good, the people will be good. The character of a ruler is like wind and that of the people is like grass. In whatever direction the wind blows, the grass always blends."[8] Chinese thought is, of course, itself composed of varying approaches to ensuring that there is harmony between the state and the people. The authorities in Beijing today, insofar as they want to invoke the tradition, would probably quote Sun Tzu's view that "man's nature is evil. Therefore the sages of antiquity . . . established the authority of rulers to govern the people, set forth clearly propriety and righteousness to transform them, instituted laws and governmental measures to rule them, and made punishments severe to restrain them, so that all will result in good order to be in accord with goodness."[9]

The common threads of the Asian philosophical tradition and historical experience are characterized by a contemporary Singaporian philosopher-statesman as "seeing order and stability as preconditions for economic growth, and growth the necessary foundation of any political order that claims to advance human dignity.... East and Southeast Asians tend to look askance on the starkly individualistic ethos of the West in which ... rights are an individual's 'trump' over the state. Most people of the region prefer the situation in which the distinctions between the individual, society, and state are less clear-cut, or at least less adversarial."[10]

However, Not Giving Up on Cosmopolitan Universalism

Respect for such diverse views and for local context in determining how to promote the world interests does not obviate the universal concerns informing the world interests nor the quest for globally collective responses to global threats and needs. Growing numbers of influential people in all countries and ethnic communities have, along with economist Amartya Sen and philosopher Kwame Anthony Appiah, a larger view of their identities than that established by domicile or place of birth. In addition to being members of particular ethnic groups (sometimes being the progeny of multicultural marriages) and citizens of particular countries, they are members and share the values of various transnational professional associations and, increasingly, transnational avocational groups. They rightly consider themselves and their cohorts citizens of the world. This growing cosmopolitan culture, which has representatives in all countries—and is persecuted in some of them—has no less a right to have its values and transnational ethos respected than do the more narrowly based cultures.[11]

Also, respect for the world's diverse cultures should not mean automatic deference to the views of the particular cultural group in control of a given state. Most countries are multicultural, and in many of them, such deference can constitute an endorsement by default of the denial of full human dignity to the members of cultural communities and indigenous peoples that hold little power in that country's polity. Social scientists, political philosophers, and statespersons have yet to devise concepts of legitimacy and practical means for penetrating the rigid rules of state sovereignty that relegate these peoples to second- or third-class status in their countries of domicile and in the world.[12]

Fostering Transnational Accountability

The central premise of the foreign policy of Higher Realism is that it is in the U.S. national interest to help transform the polyarchic global society into a world community in which threats to the healthy survival of the human species are under control, the role of force in world affairs has been reduced, poverty and disease have been significantly alleviated, the global economy is functioning well, essential ecologies are being treated with care, democracy and human rights have spread to many countries, and cultural pluralism is respected. But these interests will remain merely aspirations unless countries and peoples are accountable to one another for how they are serving or negatively affecting the world interests. Indeed, the extent to which the world approaches the desideratum of becoming a community will be crucially affected by how widely and deeply such accountability does pervade the relationships among the actors in world society, particularly the nation-states.[1] The final and capstone world interest, therefore, is transnational accountability.

The accountability norm holds that *those who can or do crucially affect the security or well-being of others (especially by inflicting harm) are answerable to those whom they immediately and directly affect and to the larger society whose well-being, norms, and behavior are implicated.*

Accountability is not the same thing as collective action, and efforts to achieve it need not be waylaid by the inherent difficulties in collective action projects—most notably the free-rider problem, which, once it is discovered to be parasitically present in a particular endeavor, can discourage even those who may have been initially enthusiastic about cooperation. But a pattern of mutual accountability in a particular realm of international activity can constitute a foundation on which to construct subsequent collective action that transcends the free-rider problem.

Given the multiplicity and crosscutting dimensions of relationships in world society, not all of the accountability obligations and processes can operate globally. Some will involve only two or three neighboring states; some—on the model of the EU—will cover whole regions or continents; and some, such as those required to deal with global warming or the stability of the international monetary system, may have to operate worldwide. The thickest accountability relationships will be functionally specific—that is, applicable to the unique problems in a particular sector.

Fortunately, there is some rudimentary scaffolding to build on in the fields of arms control, counterterrorism, international commerce, international transportation (sea and air), communications, environmental management, and human rights. In each of these realms, states and nongovernmental actors have discovered that there are often "positive sum" benefits to be achieved through institutionalized mutual accountability—even if only to establish predictability in one another's behavior and reduce the costs of fresh negotiations and transactions dispute by dispute. But new accountability processes and institutions, necessarily thin at the outset, also need to be developed to cover the inherent interdependence of various sectors—for example, trade (now mainly the province of the WTO); transborder ecologies (now primarily the responsibility of the UN Environmental Program); migration and refugee issues (the province of the UN High Commission on Refugees); and peace and security, conflict and arms control, and gross violations of the fundamental rights of peoples and persons (increasingly assigned to the often paralyzed UN Security Council). Not only at the global level but also in national government, these highly interdependent functions of governance are overly compartmentalized and frequently operate at cross-purposes. To be sure, the compartmentalization reflects the inevitable reality of particular functional agencies representing the conflicting interests in society. The need, however, no less at the international level than at the national level, is for deliberative processes to establish priorities and facilitate trade-offs among these special interests on the basis of their power to impose their will *and* on the basis of what is best for the whole society.

The transnational accountability relationships can vary along a number of dimensions: their *functional specificity* (whether they deal with one field of activity or many); the *number of participants* (whether from all countries and/or nongovernmental actors in the domain covered or just two); the *extent of constraint* on behavior (how much freedom of action is relinquished); and the *extent of institutionalization* (ranging from ad hoc, situation-specific get-togethers to permanently seated chartered organizations). At the most rudimentary level, those feeling they have been harmed by others are given opportunities to express their grievances, and those allegedly responsible for the harms and injustices are expected to explain the reasons for their actions. Higher degrees of accountability can range all the way up to institutionalized consensus rules or prohibitions on certain members of a community acting without the explicit approval of all the members.

Existing Multipurpose Regimes

The thickest and most elaborate network of transnational accountability exists in the European Union. The EU's twenty-seven nation-state members—convening in permanently seated bodies such as the European

Commission and the European Parliament and in periodic heads-of-state or ministerial meetings—are accountable to one another for their policies in many fields; in some instances, they relinquish considerable national freedom of action so as to advance the commonweal. Hardly a full-blown supranational state (and as it enlarges its membership, perhaps never destined to become one), the EU provides a laboratory for the kinds of mutual accountability among peoples that the world needs in many places in order to counteract the negative aspects of Polyarchy.

The United Nations, the largest permanently seated official international organization—comprising a multi-interest plenary body (the General Assembly), a peace- and security-focused executive (the Security Council), and numerous bodies with more specific functions—places very few constraints on the freedom of action of its members. In extreme cases, the Security Council can legally take action against member nations. But its voting rules are designed to prevent actions by the world organization that would interfere with what any of the Big Five (the United States, Russia, China, Britain, and France) or their friends would want to do. And resolutions adopted by the General Assembly and the other general membership bodies are just that—*resolutions,* without binding force unless implemented voluntarily by subsets of members who want to give teeth to these measures.

Various proposals have been floated in recent years for making the Security Council more representative of the contemporary distribution of political and economic power in the world. One way might be to bring on as "permanent members" with a veto economic powers such as Japan and Brazil and India (the latter is also now a nontrivial nuclear weapon state); another might be to add at least one influential African state and one state from the Islamic world. Other council reform proposals would add permanent members from a broader array of states, ensuring that all regions and various levels of economic development were represented.[2] Some would even take the veto away from the current Big Five. None of these proposals, however, would change the basic structure of the United Nations or render it capable of overcoming the inhibitors of collective action that are characteristic of Polyarchy.[3] More fruitful efforts to build accountability into the Polyarchy can be seen in special-purpose or functionally specific agreements and institutions.

Special-Purpose Regimes

Accountability commitments and institutions that limit nations' freedom of action in the service of greater cooperation are likely to be most successful in specialized domains, especially where there are tangible benefits to be mutually obtained or harms to be mutually avoided. Arms control is one of those fields. In this domain, a willingness to be answerable to one's rival and/or to international monitors in order to allay fears of destabilizing arms deployments can be crucial to the avoidance of expensive and counterproductive arms races. Other functionally specific domains (international communications, transportation, and fisheries, for example) have been spawning accountability regimes—minimally to keep countries, communities, and corporate entities from getting in one another's way and maximally to allocate the domain's resources among the its users.

Some Examples in the Field of Arms Control

During the Cold War, arms-control agreements crucial to the avoidance of nuclear war involved mostly bilateral accountability arrangements between the United States and the Soviet Union, including inspection and verification from reconnaissance spacecraft of their respective deployments. Similar arrangements are incorporated in the post–Cold War strategic force reduction agreements that have been negotiated between the United States and Russia. Fear that the Cold War might become a hot war as a result of misperception of one another's defensive deployments as being offensive (what academic theorists call the security dilemma) also led to the adoption of Confidence-Building Measures (CBMs) in zones of potential military clashes, such as around the border between East Germany and West Germany. In some of these arrangements, members of the opponent's military were invited into one's command headquarters to observe maneuvers or war games.

The most ambitious accountability regime in the arms-control field is the Treaty on the Nonproliferation of Nuclear Weapons (NPT), to which 189 countries are party. The NPT limits the freedom of action of the countries with nuclear weapons who belong to the regime—the United States, Russia, China, France, and Britain (India, Pakistan, Israel, and North Korea do not belong)—as well as the non-nuclear-weapon countries. The nuclear-armed countries are committed to not assisting any nation without nuclear weapons in manufacturing or otherwise acquiring nuclear weapons or nuclear explosive devices, whereas the countries without nuclear weapons are committed "not to manufacture or otherwise acquire nuclear weapons or other nuclear explosive devices; and not to seek or receive assistance in the manufacture of nuclear weapons or other nuclear explosive devices."[4]

The NPT commits the nuclear weapon countries—in return for the nonweapon countries' continuing to abstain from having their own nuclear arsenals—to help the latter develop peaceful nuclear energy programs, subject to safeguards assuring that such programs are not convertible into weapons programs. It also obliges the nuclear weapon countries "to pursue negotiations in good faith on effective measures relating to the cessation of the nuclear arms race at an early date and to nuclear disarmament, and on a treaty on general and complete disarmament under strict and effective international control."[5]

The nuclear-armed countries, operating through the Nuclear Suppliers Group, are trusted to comply with the NPT, whereas the International Atomic Energy Agency is given authority to verify, through a system of inspections and safeguards, that the non-nuclear-weapon countries are complying with their NPT commitments. It is hardly a foolproof system, since the IAEA inspections and safeguards are negotiated with each non-nuclear-weapon country, which leaves those countries wiggle room to cheat, if that is their intention (a problem encountered with Iran). Pressured by the United States, EU countries, and the IAEA Secretariat to close this loophole, many NPT members have signed "Additional Protocols" allowing IAEA inspectors even un-announced access to undeclared sites in an effort to further verify good faith compliance. Iran at first accepted such an Additional Protocol, but it subsequently renounced it because the IAEA appeared to be getting too intrusive for Tehran's comfort.

Another strongly constraining but highly specialized arms-control covenant, to which over 170 countries are parties, is the Chemical Weapons Convention. Implemented through the Organization for the Prohibition of Chemical Weapons, the CWC requires countries to allow the organization's secretariat to carry out "challenge" inspections on their territory if any other party has requested that it do so. However, most of the multilateral arms-control and confidence- and security-building measures still (but anachronistically) require that verification arrange-ments must, in each instance, be agreed to by the parties involved.

Some Examples in the Global Economy

Transnational accountability regimes have become crucial to a well-functioning global economy, as goods, money, information, and services circulate across borders at great speed—often at the speed of light. The World Trade Organization exists to ensure that countries are held ac-countable for their adherence to or deviation from the norms of reciprocity and fairness as the world economy evolves into a free and open global market. Members of the WTO agree to submit their trade disputes with one another to the organization's panels of experts and to bring their policies in line with the findings of these experts. A parallel set of accountability obligations but with more decentralized enforcement exists in the domain of monetary, banking, and currency relations to service the mutual interest in avoiding wild fluctuations of currency exchange rates and interest rates charged by central banks, which can have major disruptive impacts on vulnerable countries. The creation of the International Monetary Fund stemmed from the recognition that the market does not always provide its own correctives and that the world interest in a reasonably stable global monetary system cannot always be served by national or private bank controls on the flows of money. The IMF has become the principal auspice for constructing and maintaining multilateral consultative arrangements to steer countries away from the kind of "beggar thy neighbor" monetary and fiscal policies that can result in a worldwide constriction of trade and bring on a global economic depression.

These needed overlays of mutual accountability on the global market, administered primarily by the three institutions (the WTO, the IMF, and the World Bank), are being weakened by the political backlash against globalization. Yet paradoxically, it is these very institutions, whose mission is to husband the evolution of the global market, that have belatedly become the most important sources of moderating constraints on the sometimes overly rapid and heavy-handed efforts to push all countries—even the uncompetitive—into a survival-of-the-fittest world without economic borders. Economic globalization, driven by technology and the desire of most literate people to shop and sell in the world's markets, is here to stay—with or without its negative impacts on the well-being of many. Protectionist and xenophobic reactions against the globalization phenomenon and its institutional sponsors, plus retaliatory erections of barriers against the goods and services from countries that are moving in a protectionist direction, are likely to produce economic downturns that will further hurt those who may have been marginalized by globalization.

Accountability in the Commons

There is an obvious need and logic for mutual accountability regimes to manage environments or resources that are used but not owned by different countries—such as the oceans and other bodies of water, the atmosphere, outer space, and migratory species. And there has been considerable progress in constructing such regimes. Yet much more needs to be done to keep pace with growing problems of overuse and congestion in these realms.

Use of the Ocean

The most impressive of these commons accountability efforts, managing the ocean commons, is reflected in the Law of the Sea Treaty of 1981. (Unfortunately, this treaty is still not ratified by the United States at the time of this writing!) The increasingly clashing uses of the oceans for commercial transport, military operations, navigation, fishing, seabed resource extraction (particularly oil), coastal zone recreation, and waste disposal had to be handled in an omnibus treaty. The negotiators, to their credit, did not attempt to lock in solutions to all the problems but instead set up a flexible system of dispute-resolution processes for reconciling—in the world interest—the multifarious clashes of national special interests.

Some of the users of the ocean do, of course, operate as members of special industry groups that have their own coordination and accountability needs—the details of which are more appropriately tended to within their own international associations. One prominent globally active association of this sort is the International Maritime Organization (IMO) for sea transport. The IMO's mission is to negotiate among its members as well as with other specialized industry groups (such as oil companies engaged in seabed drilling) and international coastal and environmental protection interests over regulations on shipping at sea and in ports that are required for reasons of orderly commerce, safety, environmental protection, and peace and security. The latter function has been involving the IMO in intensive dialogue with members of the Proliferation Security Initiative—a multilateral counterterrorism effort organized by the United States for intercepting ships at sea that are suspected of carrying prohibited components of weapons of mass destruction.

Use of Airways and Outer Space

Managing issues of congestion, safety, and security against hostile actions in the airways is another mutual accountability task for which there is a lead multilateral organization, with considerable authority over what national and private carriers can do—namely, the International Civil Aviation Organization (ICAO). The congestion problem in outer space, however, particularly at the lower orbits utilized by manned spacecraft and low-flying observation and scientific satellites, begs for an authoritative regime to deal with the orbiting debris of inactive payloads, abandoned nuclear reactors, spent rockets, and tests.

Counteracting Global Warming

Finally, there is the Earth's temperate climate—the quintessential global commons. Our climate is under assault by a wide range of human activities and belatedly (not too late, it is hoped) recognized to be in need of a degree of protective care that is unlikely to be provided by the uncoordinated self-interested policies of nations and corporations. The follow-ups to the 1997 Kyoto Protocol[6]—which must now also involve the Kyoto holdouts (especially the United States, China, and India) who are the largest contributors to the greenhouse gas envelope surrounding the Earth—will require worldwide acceptance of a more deeply constraining mutual accountability regime than has ever been attempted. Higher Realism prescribes that the United States should be one of the leaders in this difficult but necessary effort.[7]

Conclusion

To the extent that such accountability norms and forms pervade world society—meaning that its members, particularly the nation-states, are answerable to one another with respect to how they are implementing or interfering with the realization of the world interests I have been discussing—the world will have become a community. This ultimate objective will not be well served, however, if the United States and other "Western" countries attempt to set up a "Concert of Democracies" outside the UN, as recommended by some prominent U.S. intellectuals, in order to "provide an alternative forum for liberal democracies to authorize collective action, including the use of force."[8] Progress toward world community is compatible with dialogue and attempts to persuade one another as to which are the best norms and forms. Such persuasion may include the credible threat that commerce, especially capital investments, will be diverted away from places where instability and conflict do not augur well for profitable returns. But progress is not compatible with attempts by a group of nations to forcibly impose their values on nonmembers, other than efforts made to counter egregious cases of brutality (such as genocide and crimes against humanity as defined in the Statute of the International Criminal Court). Progress toward world community is set back by we-they dichotomies that divide the world between good guys and bad guys. Reacting to the Concert of Democracies idea, one highly respected "non-Western" scholar observed that "no matter how any such proposal is dressed, a majority of the world's population will see that a few Western states, who represent a tiny percentage of the world's population, are still trying to impose their will on the rest of the world."[9]

Higher Realism is cognizant of the fact that the necessary mutual accountability processes and institutions will not flourish unless they are grounded in the cultural realities of Polyarchy: the identities and pride of peoples around the world in their own traditions and ways of life. Treated with respect, these identities are consistent with a cosmopolitan acceptance of also being part of the whole human community.

Improving the Policy Process

The appropriate launching pad for the new foreign policy of Higher Realism is a presidential proclamation recognizing and explaining why it is in the national interest to serve key world interests, specifically: ensuring the healthy survival of the human species, reducing the role of force, alleviating poverty and disease, maintaining a well-functioning global economy, promoting democracy and human rights, respecting cultural and religious diversity, and fostering transnational accountability. For such a foreign policy to be viable, however, it will require detailed and continuing elaboration and supervision at the highest levels of government. This will require a process designed to debate and determine priorities and trade-offs, derive the operational implications, generate the needed resources, and oversee implementation.

The design of the policy process will have to meet a number of criteria:

1. It must provide for authoritative representation—official and unofficial—of the views of those sectors of society whose inputs

and support are and will likely continue to be specially required for the programs or projects at hand.

2. It must also provide for authoritative representation of the views of communities whose security or well-being are and are likely to be significantly affected by the ongoing and contemplated policies.

3. It must directly provide the responsible decisionmakers with evaluations by professional experts (on security threats and capabilities, on the domestic and global economy, on implicated ecologies, on ethics and legality, and on the societies and cultures of implicated countries) of the views solicited under criteria 1 and 2 on required support and impacts.

Getting Broad Policy Advice

The policy formulation and implementation process for Higher Realism cannot rely mainly on intragovernmental deliberation by the U.S. president with the heads of the established departments and agencies. Nor can it rely mainly on recommendations generated by the standing interagency councils or committees (prototypically the National Security Council [NSC], the National Economic Council, or various other subcabinet committees and task groups). Policy assessments by the established government agencies are essential but insufficient for ensuring the president is properly informed, for they are often the products of interagency (and also *intra*-agency) turf battles and competition for resources that can fuse and confuse their special interests with national interests.[1] No amount of executive branch organization and reorganization is likely to fully correct for the intrusion of bureaucratic politics into what purports to be objective analysis. When presidents want to transcend the bureaucratic politics syndrome, they are well advised to reach beyond the established interagency structure in order to recruit members for ad hoc advisory groups, as President Kennedy did in composing the so-called ExCom to help him deal with the Cuban missile crisis.[2]

Whatever device a president resorts to for reducing the inevitable bureaucratic distortions (e.g., FDR's technique of making rival officials debate in front of him or Eisenhower's insistence that the agencies hammer out a common recommendation before he would meet with them in the NSC), his or her need of relevant advice will often be ill served if confined only to what can be solicited from subordinate officials—a process resulting in what political sociologist Irving Janis has labeled "groupthink."[3] George W. Bush's insular consultation style for determining his crucial foreign policy moves, such as implementing Operation Iraqi Freedom, is a notorious case in point.[4]

The high-level foreign policy consultation process should be structured to adequately tap into and funnel up to the president *non*governmental/ *private*-sector views—for this is where much of the support and resources will have to be marshaled to give the country the wherewithal to effectively pursue the Higher Realist agenda. Congress, working through its committee and specialized subcommittee hearings, can assist in the process of soliciting relevant nongovernmental views on policy options under consideration by the administration. But both the politicized selection of witnesses for these hearings as well as their testimony and interrogation, though helpful to members of Congress in crafting legislation and mobilizing votes, are not usually structured to elicit the kind of inputs needed for better-informed deliberation in the Oval Office.

Giving the Affected Early Attention

Occupational groups (say, particular segments of the labor force who feel they will be adversely affected by certain foreign trade or international environmental agreements) should not have to wait for congressional hearings on the ratification of some treaty before their concerns are taken seriously. This does not mean such groups are to be accorded a veto, as it were, on policies deemed to be in the overall national interest; this approach can, however, provide the president with timely advance warnings, while treaties are still being negotiated, of domestic political opposition that may develop down the road. In cases where it would be undesirable to alter treaty terms to accommodate such domestic concerns, the administration should at least be able to anticipate opposition and avoid being blindsided in Congress by offering the worried groups some compensation in the form of legislation regarding parallel domestic adjustment policies, including, for example, occupational adjustment training and other benefits.

If Washington is contemplating taking coercive or discriminatory international action against a nation or people considered ethnic brothers and sisters by a diaspora community living in the United States, elementary political prudence calls for inviting representatives of the affected community to meet with the president and other high officials of the administration. If the diaspora community is itself riven by political conflict, representatives of various factions should be invited, separately if necessary. Such consultations can provide an opportunity to allay concerns in the diaspora community that its members will be the victims of discriminatory treatment in the United States. It can also serve to inform the policymakers about the cultural characteristics of the foreign society they are trying to influence and that they may need to help recover from the impending conflict—knowledge that was sadly lacking in Washington at the time of the Vietnam War and, more recently, about Afghanistan, Iraq, and Iran.

Tapping the Relevant Expertise

No organizational structure will guarantee chief executives the kind of expert advice they need just when they need it. This is particularly so for the chief executive of the United States of America. President Kennedy was misadvised in standard cabinet-level meetings attended by the Joint Chiefs of Staff on how to topple Fidel Castro in the disastrous Bay of Pigs operation; afterward, he relied on ad hoc, functionally specific meetings with trusted experts, as he did with the ExCom in the missile crisis. Henry Kissinger aspired to be the provider of all the expert foreign policy advice President Nixon would need, which Kissinger would generate out of a hefty National Security Council staff pervaded by political science PhDs. But in the mid-1970s, following the Yom Kippur War, when the Arab oil cartel threatened to seriously destabilize the global economy by controlling petroleum supply and prices, Kissinger, not very well educated in economics, had to scramble for brilliant economics PhDs to add to the NSC staff. President Jimmy Carter relied too much on separate, one-on-one consultations with Secretary of State Cyrus Vance and his national security adviser, Zbigniew Brzezinski, allowing both men to think the president had fully approved their sometimes opposed strategies (which did not serve the country well in dealing with the upheaval in Iran that led to the hostage crisis at the embassy in Tehran). Ronald Reagan, trusting too much in the expertise of the CIA director, William Casey, and Colonel Oliver North at the NSC, allowed his administration to become trapped in the embarrassing Iran-contra scandal.

Despite this checkered history, and difficult as it is to do, each president must tap into a daunting range of expertise for presiding over the country's foreign policy. And each must discover and utilize a process and structure of consultation that best suits his or her decisionmaking style. Ultimately, how the system works (or fails to work) will be an expression of the personality of the president. That said, some imperatives of presidential-level deliberation with experts and guidance on who—minimally—should be invited to sit around the table can be indicated for each of the world interests discussed in the previous chapters.

Take, for example, the president's deliberations on precisely what kinds of reductions the United States can make in its strategic nuclear arsenal and how deep those reductions can go—unilaterally or in coordination with Russian reductions. In addition to consulting with the secretaries of defense, state, and treasury, with the national security adviser, and with the director of national intelligence, the president needs *direct* advice from each of the Joint Chiefs, the State Department's leading strategic arms–control negotiator, and the NSC's principal expert on strategic weapons issues. The president also must be able to sound out directly, not through reports from official subordinates, the top strategic weapons specialists at the American Federation of Scientists and the Arms Control Association, plus some of the country's top experts (in government but also in the think tanks) on Russian grand strategy and military programs.

For dealing with the problem of global warming, a mix of government officials and nongovernmental experts (the latter initially heavily involved, given the lack of a fully committed U.S. program up to the present) also must be relied on to guide the president in understanding and deciding on options. The Environmental Protection Agency lacks real clout. And the formulation of a dedicated U.S. policy for counteracting the buildup of greenhouse gases should not, at the outset, be lodged in the subcabinet or working levels at which various agencies have located responsibility for dealing with environmental issues. Washington's long-awaited serious assumption of international responsibility in this field (commensurate with the country's role as the world's leading contributor to the carbon dioxide envelope around the planet) begs for full presidential identification with the effort. Because of the scientific technicalities and the need to rebut the skeptics' lobby (which is well funded by some of the big oil companies), the president will need considerable tutelage from environmental scientists and from NGOs that have long been active on the global warming issue. Legislation probably should be introduced to create a department of the environment (which, in a Democratic administration, Al Gore might be asked to head). In the meantime, though, serious legislative or international initiatives with a reasonable chance of success will require the presidential imprimatur.

Providing the president the information and analytic wherewithal to manage the complex relationships between natural resource and ecological sustainability, economic growth and development, trade, transnational investments, interest rates, and currency values is the Herculean mandate of the three-member Council of Economic Advisers, usually chaired by a distinguished economist and assisted by a staff of about twenty-five academic economists and statisticians. Whatever advice the president receives from the council, however, must be reconciled with advice and policy demands coming from cabinet members with responsibilities strongly affected by and impacting on the national and global economy: the secretaries of treasury, state, defense, commerce, energy, agriculture, interior, transportation, labor, housing and urban development, and health and human services, plus the director of the Office of Management and Budget, the U.S. trade representative, and the administrator of the Environmental Protection Agency.

To give some coherence to policymaking in this labyrinthine structure, President Clinton created a new agency, the National Economic Council (modeled on the National Security Council) within the Executive Office of the President, to be directed by an assistant to the president for economic policy. The council is formally chaired by the president, and the regular members have included the vice president and the secretaries of the key departments, with frequent participation by the chair of the Council of Economic Advisers, the director of the Office of Management and the Budget, the U.S. trade representative, and—significantly—the national security adviser. Other attendees have been the administrator of the Environmental Protection Agency, the assistant to the president for science and technology policy, and the assistant to the president for domestic policy. Notably absent, and disappointingly so from the standpoint of Higher Realism, is a representative of the Agency for International Development (AID), a symptom of the low priority given to alleviating poverty and disease around the world—a deficiency, at the time of this writing, that needs to be corrected in the next administration.

The substantial overlap in membership between the National Economic Council and the National Security Council is indicative of the high interdependence of these two domains as well as the need to almost continually coordinate national and international economic and security policy. But what is institutionalized or formed ad hoc in order to obtain the needed expert advice and coordination of policy should not be rigidly prescribed, for to be at all useful, it must be consistent with the preferences and operating style of the president.

The interest in the agenda of Higher Realism that is the most difficult to translate into U.S foreign policy (as shown in chapter 8) is the promotion of democracy and human rights. This is because the extent to which, and when, democracy and respect for human rights can take root and flower around the world will vary from country to country, depending on the cultural soil in each place. Mistakes by the United States in attempting to push democratization and liberalization on peoples not ready for it or insisting on particular institutional forms where these are inconsistent with indigenous traditions can be avoided by adhering to the sometimes contradictory world interest in fostering respect for cultural diversity. The operationalization of the cultural diversity constraint on democracy promotion can be assisted by giving greater weight in the formulation and conduct of U.S. policy to experts on the unique histories and cultural characteristics of each country with which the United States has relations. Insofar as academics are brought into the consultation process, more opportunities should be created to tap the knowledge of anthropologists than has been the case up to now.

Finally, the transnational accountability imperative also requires more listening in Washington—by members of Congress and by policy officials—to the reports and insights of regional and country experts in academia and think tanks (such as the International Crisis Group). Policymakers also need to seek insights from government officials who have had extended tours of duty in particular foreign countries. (I have been appalled to hear from many such officials that since returning to Washington, they have found that their accumulated knowledge about the country in which they were deployed is often totally ignored, even during a brewing crisis involving that country.) To be able to bargain more effectively in multilateral arenas, U.S. diplomacy needs to be better informed about the underlying historical, sociological, cultural, and religious factors, not simply the obvious material interests, that are determining the negotiating positions of the other governments.

Determining Priorities and Trade-Offs

The policy process should be structured to facilitate the establishment of priorities and the determination of trade-offs among the eight broadly defined world interests that Higher Realism views as also being national interests of the United States. Except for the healthy survival of the human species, which is self-evidently the most highly valued world and national interest, priorities cannot be simply deduced from the substantive nature of these interests. Which of them are to be given precedence if resources to pursue them are scarce or when strategies to attain them come into conflict will have to be determined situation by situation. And even when it comes to designing policies to ensure the healthy survival of the human species—for example, by preventing a world war fought with weapons of mass destruction or avoiding a drastic heating up of the planet's climate—uncertainties about how close at hand the threat is, about the expected effectiveness and costs of alternative preventive policies, and about the urgency of initiating them will require fresh deliberation as conditions change.

Thus, the overarching national interests (and the world interests themselves) require a decisionmaking process that allows for timely and thorough examination of the interests at stake in situations that beg for a policy response—an examination conducted by the relevant stakeholders, or at least their representatives. My contention here is that an open and flexible system that encourages the president to rapidly identify and assemble, ad hoc, those stakeholders and appropriate "*dis*interested" specialists and generalists is superior to any permanently standing interagency structure that anyone has come up with thus far.

This does not preclude the establishment of standing interagency committees and/or executive-legislative commissions and task forces at various levels of the government for the continuous reformulation and monitoring of basic policies (including the allocation of responsibilities and resources) for pursuing the various world interests. Indeed, the emergence of certain conflicting priorities and the need to negotiate trade-offs are inherent in the range of interests to be pursued, and these can be usefully anticipated in the deliberations of the standing interagency bodies. Furthermore, such standing bodies can constitute a reservoir of at least some of the stakeholders and some of the expertise that may need to be quickly assembled by the president in crisis situations. Beyond that, it may be a good idea to periodically exercise this emergency response capability by conducting crisis simulation exercises.

Issues of prioritization and trade-offs to be negotiated under the Higher Realist agenda—whatever policy process organization is installed by the administration—may well involve variants of the following questions:

- Should the nonproliferation of weapons of mass destruction—a longer-term human species survival interest—take precedence over the reduction of the role of force if the threat of coercive action is deemed necessary, as a last resort, to prevent an irresponsible regime from obtaining nuclear weapons?
- What sacrifice in near-term economic prosperity is warranted to avoid the long-term costs of adjusting to the consequences of global warming?
- To what extent should major resource transfers from rich countries to poor and other free-market distorting policies be adopted in order to jump-start otherwise stalled poverty- and disease-alleviation programs?
- In order to preserve a regional balance of military power that, for the time being, has been preventing the outbreak of a major war, should the United States continue to prop up an autocratic regime against opponents who are demanding civil and political rights, including a general election (assuming that U.S. policy had been based on the expectation that if the opposition won the election, it would likely pursue an international strategy that would destabilize the regional balance of military power)?
- How tolerant, in the name of respecting cultural diversity, should the United States be of Muslim-majority developing countries that are denying fundamental rights to women?
- If gross violations of human rights approaching the level of genocide are taking place in a country but neither the United Nations nor the relevant regional multilateral organization is willing to authorize military intervention against the will of that nation's

government, should the United States intervene, assuming it has the military capability and public backing to pull off a unilateral intervention?

Clearly, such issues are not easily resolved. I make no claim that a foreign policy based on the philosophy of Higher Realism will provide the answers or an escape from the dilemmas. I am arguing, though, that the deliberations in the U.S. government and the policy community at large should be addressing such issues and policies for dealing with them from a world interest perspective; they should be asking about their impact on the overall Higher Realist imperative of furthering the evolution of the chaotic and dangerous global Polyarchy into a world community of mutual accountability. And finally, I am arguing for a policy process that provides the maximum opportunity for this world interest perspective, in all of its complexity, to be an essential part of the national foreign policy discourse.

Building Public Support

Regardless of the logic of the case for the foreign policy of Higher Realism and regardless of how convinced the president and his or her foreign policy team are that the policy and programs they have devised for its implementation serve both the U.S. interest and the world interest, neither the country nor the world will reap the benefits of the policy unless there is sufficient support in the electorate and the Congress to sustain the commitments of financial, material, and human resources that such a foreign policy will require. What, then, are the prospects for such support materializing?

The good news is that the data on public attitudes show a readiness on the part of the majority of U.S. citizens—despite recent disillusionment with how the country has conducted itself abroad—to support such a turn toward a world interest–oriented foreign policy. The bad news is that Congress tends to be more reluctant than the public to do anything for the rest of the world that could be interpreted as taking resources away from domestic projects, unless such a move is justified by an urgent need to counter threats to vital strategic U.S. interests or the country's basic economic health. Here is where the next president and members of the administration will need to take to the bully pulpit (as Teddy Roosevelt called it) to explain to the people and the politicians that *the new foreign policy need not involve substantial additional public expenditures*, with two exceptions:

- The major financial outlays that may be required to mount an all-out program to subsidize the development of non-fossil-fuel sources for the country's energy needs in order to move away from the carbon-producing greenhouse gases now responsible for global warming, and
- The funds that the country will have to commit to do its share in achieving the Millennium Development Goals for the alleviation of poverty and disease.

Moreover, the president should perhaps read aloud to the people and their representatives in Congress the results of the opinion polls showing broad popular support even for world interest initiatives that might take a proportion of the funding otherwise allocated to domestic programs.

Public Receptivity

Recent public opinion surveys refute the supposition that the people of the United States are naturally isolationist and can only be prodded by extreme international events to support their government's heavy involvement in international affairs. Increasingly, in fact, they consider themselves part of a highly interdependent world, and they are prepared to have the country contribute its fair share toward ensuring the healthy survival of the human species and the efficient and equitable use and maintenance of the planet's natural resources. They perceive this effort will necessitate controls on the availability and use of the weapons of war—especially weapons of mass destruction—and on practices that threaten Earth's crucial ecological balances, such as obtaining most of the country's energy needs from fossil fuels. In these and other dimensions of living in a progressively *materially* integrated global society, the polls indicate a potential receptivity on the part of the large majority of U.S. citizens for the Higher Realist agenda of interests and initiatives—a hunger, as it were, for leadership in Washington that, in cooperation with other countries, will take the country in that direction.

Nuclear Disarmament and Arms Control

Not surprisingly, there is solid popular support for preventing the spread of weapons of mass destruction, especially to terrorists. Yet there is considerable controversy among officials and the attentive public over the appropriate means for doing so, particularly if these would entail military action against existing or potential nuclear-armed countries that are friendly to terrorist movements. What has been surprising, and encouraging, however, is the growing support within the policy community and the public for measures to substantially reduce the reliance of the United States and other major powers on nuclear weapons for their own security.

There is now substantial public support, for example, for efforts to achieve the kind of total nuclear disarmament long called for by nuclear abolitionists such as Jonathan Schell and endorsed in 2007 by former secretaries of state George P. Shultz and Henry Kissinger, former secretary of defense William J. Perry, and the former chairman of the Senate Arms Services Committee, Sam Nunn.[1] When asked, "Assuming that there is a well-established international system for verifying that countries are complying, would you favor or oppose all countries agreeing to eliminate all of their nuclear weapons?" Seventy-three percent of a representative sample of U.S. citizens said they favored the proposal.[2] The assumption built into such proposals for reliable verification systems and universal compliance is that they would, in fact, be very difficult to achieve, but a high level of popular support for efforts to abolish the weapons that threaten the healthy survival of the human species is undeniable. The same can be said for support for steps in the *direction* of complete nuclear disarmament that may be more feasible to negotiate in the nearer term:

that is, an agreement between the United States and Russia to reduce their active nuclear weapons to a number significantly lower than the 2,000 they are committed to in existing agreements (71 percent favor this proposal),[3] and ratification by the United States of the Comprehensive (Nuclear) Test Ban Treaty (which 80 percent favor).[4]

The public also strongly supports measures to reduce the likelihood that nuclear weapons in the arsenals of the countries would ever be *used*: some 64 percent favor de-alerting all U.S. and Russian nuclear weapons, and 65 percent do not want nuclear weapons to be launched on the basis of an early warning that a nuclear attack is coming before there has been additional confirmation.[5] Some 54 percent do not want nuclear weapons used except in response to a nuclear attack, and 20 percent oppose the use of nuclear weapons "under any circumstances."[6]

There can be little doubt that the electorate will support realistic policies for assuring that weapons of mass destruction are never used in conflict and that not only will disarmament measures be seriously pursued to this effect but also that conflict escalation controls will be built into military plans and deployments.

Doing Whatever It Takes to Prevent Disastrous Global Warming

Another objective with high priority on the Higher Realist agenda— preventing the thickening of the envelope of gases surrounding the planet that is turning Earth into a greenhouse of trapped heat that will become increasingly intolerable—has also achieved a level of public support that will allow policymakers to launch major corrective initiatives, even very expensive ones. The latest comprehensive surveys of public opinion on the problem show 86 percent affirming that the United States should limit greenhouse gases and 94 percent saying that the country should be doing at least as much as others are, such as the European nations. So-called cap-and-trade initiatives presently have the highest levels of support (each of the three leading candidates for the presidency in the spring of 2008 offered such schemes), with 83 percent of the respondents being in favor of legislation requiring large companies to reduce their greenhouse gas emissions to 1990 levels by 2020. And very large majorities support giving tax incentives to utility companies that sell environmentally clean energy and to individuals who buy energy-efficient appliances. Also, more than 75 percent support a requirement that all new automobiles be hybrid electric or otherwise configured to drastically reduce gas consumption.[7] Accomplishing the latter purpose via a major tax increase on gasoline, with the revenue earmarked to subsidize innovations—say, for the capturing of solar energy—was still regarded as a political hot potato in 2008, but other poll results suggest the people might be ready for this kind of "sacrifice" in the service of the long-term goal of preventing disastrous global warming. An August 2007 poll asked: "From what you know about the actions this country might take to address climate change and reduce global warming, do you think the costs would be unacceptably high, or it can be done without taking on high economic costs, or the economic costs would be high but worth the circumstances?" Results showed that 27 percent thought what was needed could be done without high costs; 17 percent said that the sacrifice would be too high; and 42 percent responded that the costs would be high "but worth it." (Some 14 percent were unsure.)[8] All in all, these results show that the national constituency for starting to take big steps now to abate the global warming trend, even if this involves incurring significant costs, is considerably larger than the constituency for gradualist or wait-and-see approaches. Politicians take note!

Contributing Resources for Alleviation of Poverty and Disease

Because it requires nontrivial financial outlays, a serious effort to alleviate extreme poverty and disease around the world has been a political nonstarter. But with respect to this world interest, too, there has been a discernible shift in attitude on the part of the U.S. public. Surveys since the year 2000 show that upwards of 85 percent support providing food and medical assistance to people in needy countries.[9] The majority still favors giving higher priority to programs for combating poverty domestically than to foreign programs. When asked what percentage of their tax dollars that go to helping poor people at home and abroad should be devoted to helping those in other countries, the mean response was 16 percent. Moreover, when asked if they would be willing to pay an additional $50 a year in taxes to combat poverty abroad, 75 percent said yes.

The most striking finding in these public opinion surveys is about the *reasons* for sending aid abroad. Some 34 percent selected the conventionally respected response: "We should only send aid to parts of the world where the US has security interests." But a surprising 63 percent selected the statement: "When hunger is a major problem in some part of the world we should send aid whether or not the US has a security interest in that region."[10] And consistent with this relative downgrading of security interests, a solid majority preferred giving the aid through multilateral institutions rather than bilaterally. Most respondents also indicated a preference for assistance programs that were designed to counter the sources of the poverty and not just provide food and medical help to suffering populations. Thus, for this aspect of the Higher Realist agenda, too, there is a receptive public waiting for an administration in Washington to seize the initiative and for Congress to provide the wherewithal to service the national and world interests.

How Much Accountability to Others?

Another crucial feature of the proposed foreign policy that might seem to face an uphill battle in generating the required public and congressional support is the prescription for enhanced transnational accountability processes and institutions for serving the various public goods and world interests that are on the agenda of Higher Realism. But the widely held assumption that the American people are unwilling to cede any of their country's sovereignty to transnational or supranational levels of governance also needs revision in light of the polling data. Thus, a WorldPublicOpinion.org poll of October 2006 found that 69 percent agreed with the following proposition: "As the world becomes more interconnected, and problems such as terrorism and the environment are of a more international nature, it will be increasingly necessary for the US to work through international institutions."[11] Furthermore, in a related poll, about 75 percent of the people who responded wanted the United States to be a participating member of the International Criminal Court (unlike President George W. Bush, who "unsigned" the international statute that President Clinton had signed but was reluctant to ask the Senate to ratify)—another indication that the elected representatives tend to exaggerate the reluctance of the country to be transnationally accountable for its behavior.[12]

The Nation Is Ready for a Foreign Policy of Higher Realism: Will Its Leaders Seize the Opportunity?

I am not arguing that policy should be made by opinion polls. "There goes the crowd. I am their leader. I must follow them!" is not the presidential posture the country needs or is asking for. Rather, I have invoked the data on public attitudes to show that the nation is ready—despite the recent hubristic delusions of omnipotence and omniscience—to have its leaders participate fully in the Higher Realist project of transforming the increasingly polyarchic global society into a world community of mutual responsibility and accountability.

To participate fully in this project—the last thing even those who have resented U.S. hegemonism want is for the United States to retreat into isolationism—U.S. leaders will need to reconceptualize the national interests as being thickly intertwined with the world interests I have outlined. I have set out the basic parameters for the foreign policy that such a reconceptualization of national interests implies, and I have stated some of my preferences for particular ways of implementing that basic foreign policy.

The recommended policies are not the only ones that can be derived from the premises of Higher Realism. They are offered mainly as illustrations of how this way of thinking about world politics opens up

U.S. policy alternatives that may have been prematurely dismissed as "unrealistic." The policy options are meant to draw attention to new possibilities for simultaneously serving world interests and the country's national interests.

Future generations will look back at those who assumed responsibility for U.S. foreign policy in 2009 and assess the job they did. Will these policymakers, like their predecessors in the 1940s, be judged as having risen to the challenge of a new era?

When in the Course
of Human Events . . .

T he words kept rebounding in my head long after the dissipation of the glare and smoke from the rockets that had been
exploded in celebration of the 232nd anniversary of the eloquent
Declaration of Independence: "When in the course of human events it
becomes necessary for one people to dissolve the political bonds which
have connected them with another . . . " Back at my computer, staring at
the keyboard, wondering if the arguments would flow more persuasively
were I using a quill pen instead, I was convinced, as Jefferson and his
colleagues were, that this was a time in the course of human events to
remedy the mismatch between the supposedly sovereign polity and the
economy and between that polity and the ecology, consistent with the
changing identifications among the world's peoples. But now the remedy
would have to be very different.

When the Declaration was penned, the lack of congruence in North
America between the dominant polity—the British Empire—and the
actual patterns of economic and social life among the British subjects in

the thirteen colonies moved the believers in political self-determination to a courageous insistence on separation. Today, by contrast, believers in governance responsive to the informed will of the people face a growing problem of polity-society incongruence in the structure of the world polity itself: most of the nearly 200 nation-states (the majority of them the products of successful national self-determination movements against their colonial overlords) are reluctant to dilute their own internationally recognized sovereignty over the people within their jurisdictions. Yet many of the dire threats to the security and well-being of their peoples cannot be countered without a major expansion of transnational and supranational cooperation—some of which must substantially limit national sovereign prerogatives.

Perhaps we need a Declaration of *Inter*dependence to drive home awareness of the gap between what is required to effectively counter the transnational threats to human security and well-being and the capacity of the state and nonstate institutions of the polyarchic system to generate the needed corrective action and public goods. But what would that Declaration prescribe? Certainly, it would not call for a dissolution of the existing nation-states and the transferring of sovereignty and citizens' loyalties to a unitary world state, for that would be at too much tension with the historically evolved norms and forms of human society. To peaceably accommodate the world's diverse cultures, the laws emanating from such a unitary state would have to be so ambiguously written as to render effective and accountable governance impossible; rather, there would be huge opportunities for corrupt implementation. But an overriding of the deeply ingrained cultural diversity in the service of a unitary system of laws could not be accomplished without massive coercion—world war to bring it into being and civil wars to keep it intact—that would be incompatible with the humane values such a revolutionary transformation would have been designed to serve.

A Declaration of Interdependence consistent with Higher Realism's analyses and prescriptions would not flatly reject the emergent global polity of Polyarchy. It would recognize and flexibly accommodate many of Polyarchy's diverse norms and forms—including the persisting crucial importance of nation-states as legitimate agents for rule-making and rule enforcement. But it would insist on subjecting the nation-states and other powerful actors in the global polity—subnational, transnational, governmental, and nongovernmental—to reliable mutual accountability processes and obligations congruent with the patterns of their interdependence. Those patterns of interdependence and the accountability arrangements that are needed to establish such congruence comprise the set of world interests (which are also in the U.S. interest) that I have analyzed in the previous chapters. Under Higher Realism, U.S. policies would be evaluated and decided upon according to whether, and to what extent, they enhanced or undermined these world interests.

Encouraging Signs

This book went to press amid signs that serious discourse among policy influentials, looking toward the institution of a new foreign policy with the inauguration of the next U.S. administration, was moving in the direction of Higher Realism. Neither the leading candidates for president in 2008 nor their principal foreign policy spokespersons could be expected to fully and openly embrace the philosophy and its tenets during the election campaign. But even their sound bite–constrained rhetoric reflected a growing recognition of the polyarchic complexities to which the nation must adapt and the ways in which the security and well-being of the people of the United States have become inextricably intertwined with the security and well-being of peoples around the globe.

Significantly, mainline foreign policy journals have featured articles challenging not only the clearly outdated premise that the United States is the unipolar superpower around which most others in the system must gravitate but also the recently fashionable view that the postunipolar world is multipolar. "Be careful what you wish for," wrote Niall Ferguson in *Foreign Policy*. "The alternative to unipolarity would not be multipolarity at all. It would be apolarity—a global vacuum of power. And far more dangerous forces than rival great powers would benefit from such a not-so-new world order."[1] Closely echoing my writings on Polyarchy, Richard Haass, the president of the Council on Foreign Relations, in a *Foreign Affairs* article titled "The Age of Nonpolarity," observed that "today's world differs in a fundamental way from one of classic multipolarity: there are many more power centers, and quite a few of these poles are not nation-states. Indeed, one of the cardinal features of the contemporary international system is that nation-states have lost their monopoly on power and in some domains their preeminence as well. States are being challenged from above, by regional and global organizations; from below, by militias; and from the side, by a variety of nongovernmental organizations (NGOs) and corporations. Power is now found in many hands and in many places."[2] More optimistic than Ferguson with respect to the implications for global governance, Haass envisioned much of the world's necessary multilateral cooperation taking place via coalitions whose membership would vary with who the important stakeholders were on particular issues.

Even on the part of the Bush administration during its final year in office, there were indications of adaptations—however reluctant—to at least some of the realities (such as the difficulties in democratizing Iraq) that had shattered the illusions of U.S. omnipotence and omniscience in the neoconservative agenda. Typical was posture assumed by the national security adviser, Stephen Hadley, honoring the work of the United States Institute of Peace, as he averred how the Bush administration was working for peace and freedom cooperatively—often multilaterally—and with respect for cultural diversity. Strengthening the institutions of liberty, he said, "does not mean imposing our own form of these institutions upon them. In many nations, these institutions will look quite different from those in the United States. They will reflect the unique history and culture of the nations themselves. Yet these institutions are necessary to give the people of these nations the realistic hope of a better life and to help strengthen the resistance of those nations to the transnational threats of the 21st century."[3]

It was also revealing to hear Secretary of Defense Robert Gates explicitly embrace the concept of "soft power" and call for "a dramatic increase in spending on the civilian instruments of national security—diplomacy, strategic communications, foreign assistance, civic action, and economic reconstruction and development.... We must focus our energies beyond the guns and steel of the military, beyond just our brave soldiers, sailors, Marines, and airmen. We must also focus our energies on the other elements of national power that will be so crucial in the coming years."[4]

And then there were the belated efforts of Secretary of State Condoleezza Rice to refurbish her reputation as a Realist. Having begun her public policy career with that academic credential, Rice had become a favorite target for criticisms from former colleagues when, as national security adviser, she metamorphosed into a neoconservative apparatchik. Now, approaching the end of her government tenure and over the objections of holdouts such as Vice President Cheney, she appeared more willing to communicate (if not formally negotiate) with the world's "rogues" and tyrants (in Pyongyang, Tehran, even Gaza) if that could avert a dangerous escalation of conflict. Yet in an article defensively titled "Rethinking the National Interest: American Realism for a New World," Secretary Rice was still transparently ambivalent when it came to the priority to be given in U.S. foreign policy to democratization over conflict resolution—wanting to hang on to the neoconservative mantra that "democratic state building is now an urgent component of our national interest," while granting that some of our most "capable friends" in fighting terrorism and sustaining a range of geopolitical interests "are often not democratic."[5]

As encouraging as these signs might be for a renaissance of Realism, they point more in the direction of Conventional Realism than toward Higher Realism. They emphasize mostly how to adapt prudentially to the messy present, not wanting to see the country embarrassed again by policies that might smack of world-transforming idealism. But this would be an overreaction to the hubris of the recent past, for the world interests that, because of their indispensability to the country's national interests, must be seriously pursued—ensuring the healthy survival of the human species, reducing the role of force, alleviating poverty and disease, maintaining a well-functioning global economy, arresting disturbances to global ecologies, promoting democracy and human rights, respecting cultural diversity, fostering transnational accountability—involve policies that, even during the process of implementing them, will be world-transforming.

From World Society to World Community

A society—a collection of beings who are dependent on one another for sustenance and basic amenities—evolves into a community as its members, recognizing their vital interdependence, commit themselves to mutual assistance in achieving the general welfare and countering threats to one another's security and well-being. That recognition and the commitments it spawns, if they are taken seriously and translated into mutual accountability arrangements, even though the practical policy implications may be hotly disputed, are themselves indicators of the existence of an embryonic community waiting to be born.

This book has documented both the reality and the growing recognition of the interdependence of the people on Earth—with one another and with the planet's natural ecologies. And it has, through developing the concept of world interests, argued on behalf of translating that recognition into the commitments that would transform world society into a mutually accountable and mutually caring world community. Higher Realism prescribes that the United States should be not just "present at the creation" of such a world community out of the existing world society but also an active facilitator of its birth and an attentive nurturer of its development.

Astronauts looking at our planet from outer space have been moved to reflect on its beauty *and* its possibly precarious fate. The rest of us can attempt to simulate the experience by viewing reconnaissance-satellite photos. But in whatever way this dramatic perspective registers in our minds, it validates the Higher Realist paradigm of Earth, despite its inherently pluralistic polity, being one world—physically, geologically, ecologically, and now technologically—that its human inhabitants must learn to jointly care for in their common interest.

Notes

Notes for Introduction

1. Joseph S. Nye, *Soft Power: The Means to Success in World Politics* (New York: Public Affairs, 2004).

2. I have adapted the concept of *polyarchy* (a term coined by political scientist Robert Dahl to describe patterns of participation and opposition in domestic politics) to denote an essentially leaderless pattern of world politics featuring many different kinds of actors and power—governmental and nongovernmental—characterized by diverse and volatile alignments and adversary relationships. As such, with respectful apologies to Dahl, since he gave us the term, my usage is somewhat more etymologically correct. See Robert A. Dahl, *Polyarchy: Particpation and Opposition* (New Haven, CT: Yale University Press, 1971).

Notes for Chapter One

1. Madeleine Albright, interview on NBC's *Today Show*, February 19, 1998.

2. Remarks by Vice President Dick Cheney before the Council on Foreign Relations, February 15, 2002, available at www.whitehouse.gov/vicepresident/news-speeches.

3. George W. Bush, *The National Security Strategy of the United States* (Washington, DC: White House, September 20, 2002).

4. President George W. Bush, "Remarks on the Twentieth Anniversary of the National Endowment for Democracy, November 2, 2003," text in the *New York Times*, November 6, 2003.

5. An early and widely cited expression of the unipolar thesis was Charles Krauthammer, "The Unipolar Moment," *Foreign Affairs: America and the World 1990/91* 70, no 1, special issue (Winter 1990–1991): 23–33. See also Michael Mastanduno, "Preserving the Unipolar Moment: Realist Theories and Grand Strategy after the Cold War," *International Security* 21, no. 4 (Spring 1997): 49–98.

6. For the current and projected size and composition of U.S. military forces, see the annual Department of Defense budget request to Congress, available at www .defenselink.mil. Despite the strain on U.S. military resources in Afghanistan and Iraq, the overwhelming U.S. military superiority remains dramatic and unprecedented, and the deployment of U.S. forces in more than 100 countries around the world, though thinned out due to operations in Iraq, remains unrivaled. For information on the U.S. strategic nuclear arsenal, see Congressional Research Service, *U.S. Strategic Nuclear Forces: Background and Developments* (CRS Report for Congress, September 2007), available at www.opencrs.com. The assessment by Stephen G. Brooks and William C. Wohlforth, "American Primacy in Perspective," *Foreign Affairs* 81, no. 4 (July–August 2002): 20–33, is still widely regarded as an irrefutable characterization of overall U.S. power.

7. Central Intelligence Agency, *World Factbook,* available at www.cia.gov, accessed on February 25, 2008.

8. Agency for International Development, available at www.usaid.gov/policy/budget, accessed on June 29, 2008.

9. In the academic literature on international systems, there is no agreed-upon definition of the *-polar* suffix in the bipolar, multipolar, and unipolar typology. Thus, Kenneth Waltz, in *Theory of International Politics* (Boston: Addison Wesley, 1979), pp. 161–193, used it simply to designate the *number* of powerful states in a system, whereas Raymond Aron, in *Peace and War: A Theory of International Relations* (New York: Praeger, 1966), pp. 125–149, compared systems divided into two camps (bipolar) with systems having numerous power centers (multipolar), some of which may operate as coalitions and some of which may be states standing apart from any coalitions. Standard contemporary textbooks reflect the confusion. For example, Joshua Goldstein, in *International Relations* (New York: Longman, 2003), pp. 98–99, stated that "in a multipolar system there are typically five or six centers of power, which are not grouped into alliances. Each state participates independently and on relatively equal terms with the others.... A bipolar system has two predominant states or two great rival alliances.... [A] unipolar system has a single center of power around which all others revolve."

10. Even most of the professedly nonaligned countries tilted rather obviously to one side or the other during most of the Cold War: for example, Egypt leaned toward the Soviet Union and Mexico toward the United States. India, widely regarded as the leader of the nonaligned movement, though never really taking orders from Moscow also tended to take the Kremlin's side in many Cold War disputes.

11. John Mearsheimer, *The Tragedy of the Great Powers* (New York: Norton, 2001).

12. For additional discussion of how the characteristics and roles of hegemonic powers affect the prospects for peace and war, see Robert Gilpin, *War and Change in International Politics* (Cambridge: Cambridge University Press, 1981); Stephen Krasner, "State and Power and the Structure of International Trade," *World Politics* 28, no. 3 (April 1976): 317–347; and Timothy McKeown, "Hegemonic Stability Theory and Nineteenth-Century Tariff Levels in Europe," *International Organization* 37 (Winter 1983): 73–91.

13. For discussion of China's power, ambitions, and problems, see Evan S. Medeiros and M. Taylor Fravel, "China's New Diplomacy," *Foreign Affairs* 82, no. 6 (November–December 2003): 22–35. See also Thomas Christensen, "Posing Problems without Catching Up: China's Rise and Challenges for U.S. Security Policy," *International Security* 25, no. 4 (Spring 2001): 5–40.

14. For analysis of Japanese interests and capabilities, see, for example, Eric Heginbotham and Richard Samuels, "Japan's Dual Hedge," *Foreign Affairs* 81, no. 5 (September–October 2002): 110–121. An assessment of the prospects for a more assertive, even militarized, Japanese diplomacy in reaction to what I call Polyarchy appears in Eugene Matthews, "Japan's New Nationalism," *Foreign Affairs* 82, no. 6 (November–December 2003): 74–90.

15. Seyom Brown, *New Forces, Old Forces, and the Future of World Politics* (New York: HarperCollins, 1995).

16. Such cross pressures on and within the U.S.- and Soviet-led alliances did, of course, exist during the Cold War—most dramatically in the 1956 British-French-Israeli military assault on Egypt, surprising and angering the Eisenhower administration; in France's acquisition of its own nuclear arsenal following that assault; and in China's unilateral expansionary moves against Taiwan and on the Sino-Indian border (crises in which the Kremlin failed to back Beijing against U.S. threats), leading to China's development of its own nuclear weapons in the 1960s. But during that era, such defections from superpower control were widely recognized as having the potential of dangerously collapsing the constraints the bipolar system provided against the outbreak of a planet-destroying World War III. By contrast, in the emergent Polyarchy, although there are fewer disincentives to alliance defection and unilateral action, the likelihood is remote that such moves, even if they precipitate local war, will engulf the whole system in another world war.

17. Department of Defense, *2001 Quadrennial Defense Review Report* (Washington, DC: Department of Defense, 2001), p. 43.

18. International Commission on Intervention and State Sovereignty, *The Responsibility to Protect* (Ottawa: International Development Research Center), p. xi.

19. The neoconservative version of Pax Americana was promulgated as national policy in George W. Bush, *The National Security Strategy of the United States* (Washington, DC: White House, September 20, 2002), and reiterated in numerous speeches by high administration officials. Bush gave its neo-Wilsonian content stirring articulation in his second inaugural address, on January 20, 2005, proclaiming, "The survival of liberty in our land increasingly depends on the success of liberty in other lands," and promising, "When you stand for liberty, we will stand with you." The address is available at www.whitehouse.gov. A scholarly analysis of influential neoconservatives is provided by Stefan Halper and Jonathan Clarke, *America Alone: The Neo-conservatives and the Global Order* (Cambridge: Cambridge University Press, 2004). For an analysis of how the ideas became dominant in the Bush administration, see James Mann, *Rise of the Vulcans: The History of Bush's War Cabinet* (New York: Viking, 2004). The *Weekly Standard*, edited by William Kristol, is the most prominent neoconservative magazine. And in the think tank world, the Heritage Foundation and the American Enterprise Institute are preeminent centers of neoconservative policy analysis and prescription.

20. David Skidmore, "Understanding the Unilateralist Turn in U.S. Foreign Policy," *Foreign Policy Analysis* 2 (2005): 207–228.

21. Six years after President George H. W. Bush, victorious in the Gulf War effort to expel Saddam Hussein from Kuwait, proclaimed an end to the "Vietnam syndrome," *International Security* published as its lead article a strongly articulated argument for pulling U.S. military forces out of Europe and Asia and substantially scaling down the U.S. military presence, particularly of its ground forces, in the Middle East. The end of the Cold War, the article contended, made these very expensive deployments anachronistic. The authors were not urging economic disengagement from the world or political indifference to violations of human rights. But they contended that the only justification for a continuation of America's global military engagement would be "some new ambitious strategy—to prevent war everywhere, to make everyone democratic, or to keep everyone else down. But if Americans simply want to be free, enjoy peace, and concentrate more on problems closer to home, the choice is clear: it is time to come home, America." See Eugene Gholz, Daryl G. Press, and Harvey M. Sapolsky, "Come Home, America: The Strategy of Restraint in the Face of Temptation," *International Security* 21, no. 4 (Spring 1997): 4–49.

22. See, for example, Chalmers Johnson, *The Sorrows of Empire: Militarism, Secrecy, and the End of the Republic* (New York: Metropolitan, 2004); John B. Judis, *The Folly of Empire: What George W. Bush Could Learn from Theodore Roosevelt and Woodrow Wilson* (New York: Scribner's, 2004); and Ivan Eland, *The Empire Has No Clothes: U.S. Foreign Policy Exposed* (Washington, DC: Independence Institute, 2004).

23. The publication of Samuel P. Huntington's *Who Are We? The Challenges to American National Identity* (New York: Simon and Schuster, 2004), can be viewed as a

sign of the contemporary market (which is perhaps growing) for intellectual and social science justifications for the new isolationism.

24. I have lumped together Classical Realism and its various Neorealist offshoots under the heading "Conditional Realism" because for purposes of the present analysis, their common basic assumptions about the anarchic international system and the preoccupation of the system's principal actors (the leading nation-states) with the international distribution of coercive power distinguish this worldview from the others, including what I call Higher Realism. Although the so-called Offensive Realists (à la John Mearsheimer) may differ in some of their analytical premises and policy prescriptions from the so-called Defensive Realists (à la Robert Jervis), the response to Polyarchy I have sketched in this section can flow from their shared insistence that the parameters of world politics in any era, and therefore the range of rational foreign policy alternatives for a country such as the United States, are largely defined by the relative power of the major states vis-à-vis one another. I further distinguish Conventional Realism from Higher Realism in chapter 2.

25. See, for example, Robert J. Art, *A Grand Strategy for America* (Ithaca, NY: Cornell University Press, 2003). Art also gives high priority to preventing "great power Eurasian wars and, if possible, the intense security competitions that make them possible," and therefore, he also recommends a continued substantial deployment of U.S. forces in Europe and Asia. Other Realists are somewhat more restrictive in their selection of U.S. interests worth fighting for and of the military implications. Thus, Stephen M. Walt, in *Taming American Power: The Global Response to U.S. Primacy* (New York: Norton, 2005), argues against continuing to maintain substantial deployments of U.S. troops in Europe and Asia during peacetime and instead advocates a strategy of "offshore balancing."

26. Barry Posen has suggested that a U.S. military capable of maintaining command of the oceans, outer space, and airspace above 5,000 meters is sufficient to support a Realist, even hegemony-preserving, foreign policy. Command of these global "commons" areas means that the United States can credibly threaten to deny their use to others and that others would lose a military contest if they attempted to deny any of the commons to the United States. See his "Command of the Commons: The Military Foundation of U.S. Hegemony," *International Security* 28, no. 1 (June 2003): 5–46.

27. The concept of the "irreducible national interest" was developed in Seyom Brown, *The Faces of Power: Constancy and Change in United States Foreign Policy from Truman to Clinton* (New York: Columbia University Press, 1994), pp. 3–4.

28. Hans J. Morgenthau, *Politics among Nations: The Struggle for Power and Peace*, 5th ed. (New York: Alfred A. Knopf, 1973), pp. 554–555. The contemporary Conventional Realists are also in tune with Morgenthau's first fundamental rule: "Diplomacy must be divested of the crusading spirit" (551–552).

29. See, for example, John J. Mearsheimer and Stephen M. Walt, "An Unnecessary War," *Foreign Policy* (January–February 2003): 50–59. This article was written at the time it was still generally assumed that Saddam Hussein did have weapons of mass destruction.

30. For many of these statements, visit the Coalition for Realistic Foreign Policy's Web site, www.realisticforeign policy org.

31. The "constructivist" school of international relations, criticizing the Realist view as static, is all in favor of system transformation—but perhaps too optimistically, in its assumption that a sufficient density and intensity of interactions among actors can lead to system transformation. See, for example, Alexander Wendt, "Anarchy Is What States Make of It," *International Organization* 46, no. 3 (Spring 1992): 391–425; and Dale Copeland, "The Constructivist Challenge to Structural Realism, *International Security* 25, no. 2 (Fall 2000): 187–212.

32. Some analysts with claims to Realist credentials are now supporting this view. Thus, John Ikenberry has urged the United States to champion and participate in the building of a global "constitutional" order in which "power is exercised—at least to some extent—through agreed-upon institutional rules and practices, thereby limiting the capacities of states to exercise power in arbitrary and indiscriminate ways or use their power advantages to gain a permanent advantage over weaker states." See G. John Ikenberry, *After Victory: Institutions, Strategic Restraint, and the Rebuilding of Order after Major Wars* (Princeton, NJ: Princeton University Press, 2001), p. 19. And Richard Haass argues that the increasingly "integrated" world of the twenty-first century requires institutions to constructively manage the integration. The foreign policy debate, he writes, "ought not to be whether to choose unilateralism or multilateralism, but how to choose wisely among the various forms of the latter, that is, when to turn to the UN as opposed to other standing clusters of states, alliances, regional groupings, contact groups, or ad hoc coalitions of the willing. The guiding principle should be to aim for forms of cooperation that are as broad and as formal as possible—and to choose narrow (less inclusive) and informal forms of cooperation only as required." See Richard N. Haass, *The Opportunity: America's Moment to Alter History's Course* (New York: Public Affairs, 2005), p. 200. For a conceptual scholarly analysis of the various means (and difficulty) of enhancing international accountability processes and institutions, see Ruth W. Grant and Robert O. Keohane, "Accountability and the Abuses of Power in World Politics," *American Political Science Review* 99, no. 1 (February 2005): 29–43.

33. As put by one sage analyst, "A dominant power like the United States is apt to find multilateral cooperation restraining. Possessing extensive policy options—including unilateralism, bilateral arrangements, or temporary coalitions—it can often afford (at least in the short term) to bypass consultations, enforce its will, or absorb the costs of acting alone." See Stewart Patrick, "Multilateralism and Its Discontents: The Causes

and Consequences of U.S. Ambivalence," in Stewart Patrick and Shepard Forman, eds., *Multilateralism and U.S. Foreign Policy: Ambivalent Engagement* (Boulder, CO: Lynne Rienner, 2002), pp. 1–46.

34. John Ikenberry has observed a similar phenomenon, namely, two basic types of alternative strategies being pursued vis-à-vis the United States. First are the "strategies of resistance," including "buffering" to reduce the direct influence of the United States by inducing it to rely for the issue at hand on multilateral institutions or processes; "baiting," by creating such multilateral venues despite U.S. objections and thereby making it harder for the United States to oppose one's policies; and "bargaining," by offering or withholding cooperation with the United States in exchange for U.S. responsiveness to one's preferences. And second are the "strategies of engagement," involving working with the United States in ways that create a degree of U.S. dependence on one's cooperation so as to avoid having the United States exploit or take one for granted. See G. John Ikenberry, "Strategic Reactions to American Preeminence: Great Power Politics in the Age of Uncertainty," *Report to the National Intelligence Council*, July 28, 2003, p. 3, available at www.cia.gov/nic/confreports. Similarly, Stephen Walt had pointed to a range of strategies, other than simple bandwagoning or balancing, that are being pursued by other countries to deal with what they believe to be otherwise overbearing U.S. power. On the one hand, there are cooperative strategies of accommodation, including quid pro quo agreements in which the United States agrees to support one's local interests; personal "bonding" by one's leaders with U.S. leaders (e.g, Blair with Bush) so as to bring home some payoffs for one's constituents; mutual support for each other's special interests; and "penetration" of the U.S. political system through mobilization of active lobbying groups (such as the American supporters of Israel) to obtain advantages for one's country. On the other hand, there are strategies of opposition, including "balancing" (of which Walt found strikingly little in the current international system); "delegitimation," by portraying U.S. policies as violating international law or norms; "blackmail," in threatening unwanted actions to extract concessions (such as North Korea's acceleration of its nuclear weapons program); and "asymmetric" responses (terrorism being the most stark example). See Walt, *Taming American Power*.

Notes for Chapter Two

1. The Classical Realists are carefully analyzed by Michael Joseph Smith, *Realist Thought from Weber to Kissinger* (Baton Rouge: Louisiana State University Press, 1986). The Neorealists are well represented, and criticized, in Robert O. Keohane, ed., *Neorealism and Its Critics* (New York: Columbia University Press, 1986). For the Structural Realists, see Barry Buzan, Charles Jones, and Richard Little, *The Logic of*

Anarchy: Neorealism and Structural Realism (New York: Columbia University Press, 1993). The principal case for Offensive Realism is made by John Mearsheimer, *The Tragedy of Great Power Politics* (New York: Norton, 2001).

2. International Task Force on Global Public Goods, *Meeting Global Challenges: International Cooperation in the National Interest* (Stockholm: International Task Force on Global Public Goods, 2006). See also Scott Barrett, *Why Cooperate? The Incentive to Supply Global Public Goods* (New York: Oxford University Press, 2007). An earlier elucidation of the concept was provided by Charles P. Kindleberger, "International Public Goods without International Government," *American Economic Review* 76, no. 1 (March 1986): 1–13.

Notes for Chapter Three

1. R. P. Turco, A. B. Toon, T. P. Ackerman, J. B. Pollack, and C. Sagan, "Nuclear Winter: Global Consequences of Multiple Nuclear Explosions," *Science* 222, no. 4630 (December 23, 1983).

2. Ibid. It should be noted that there have been lively debates among scientists as to the methodology and validity of such nuclear winter studies. However, when it comes to the bottom line of what kind of risks to human survival can be anticipated from large-scale nuclear war, the differences are over the magnitude and geographic extent of the catastrophic effects, not whether they will be catastrophic for human health and well-being across very large areas of the globe. See Brian Martin, "Nuclear Winter: Science and Politics," *Science and Public Policy* 15, no. 5 (October 1988): 321–334.

3. Winston Churchill delivered this famous "balance of terror" aphorism in his defense policy speech of January 3, 1955, *House of Commons Parliamentary Debates* [Hansard], 5th series, vol. 537 (London: House of Commons, 1985).

4. Excerpts from "Nuclear Posture Review Report," Department of Defense submission to Congress, December 31, 2001, published by Global Security Org at www.globalsecurity.org/wmd/library/policy/dod/npr, accessed on June 30, 2008.

5. The original formulation of the security dilemma concept was developed by John Herz in his *Political Realism and Political Idealism* (Chicago: University of Chicago Press, 1951). For elaboration, see Robert Jervis, *Perception and Misperception in World Politics* (Princeton, NJ: Princeton University Press, 1976).

6. Office of the Secretary of Defense, *Annual Report to Congress: Military Power of the People's Republic of China* (Washington, DC: Department of Defense, 2008).

7. "China's Military Space Strategy: An Exchange [between Ashley Tellis, Michael Krepon, Eric Hagt, Shen Dingli, Bao Shixiu, and Michael Pillsbury]," *Survival* 50, no. 1 (February–March 2008): 157–198.

8. For more on the underlying systemic determinants of such competitive military buildups, see John Meirsheimer, *The Tragedy of Great Power Politics* (New York: Norton, 2001).

9. I detailed the ways in which conservative fiscal policy considerations were responsible for the nuclear emphasis in the Eisenhower administration's military strategy in *The Faces of Power: Constancy and Change in United States Foreign Policy from Truman to Clinton* (New York: Columbia University Press, 1994).

10. I analyzed this early cynical game of U.S.-Soviet competition with grandiose but totally unrealistic nuclear disarmament plans in ibid., pp. 22–23. Truman quoted himself on how Baruch should play the disarmament game in his *Memoirs: Years of Trial and Hope* (New York: Doubleday, 1956), p. 11.

11. "Treaty on the Non-proliferation of Nuclear Weapons."

12. The case for a total abolition of nuclear weapons was strongly represented by Jonathan Schell in his *Seventh Decade: The New Shape of Nuclear Danger* (New York: Metropolitan, 2007).

13. George P. Shultz, Henry A. Kissinger, William J. Perry, and Sam Nunn, "A World Free of Nuclear Weapons," *Wall Street Journal,* January 4, 2007. The statement in this op-ed piece was endorsed by Martin Anderson, Steve Andreasen, Michael Armacost, William Crowe, James Goodby, Thomas Graham Jr., Thomas Henriksen, David Holloway, Max Kampelman, Jack Matlock, John McLaughlin, Don Oberdorfer, Rozanne Ridgway, Henry Rowen, Roald Sagdeev, and Abraham Sofaer.

14. Schell, *Seventh Decade,* pp. 213–214.

15. Michael Quinlan, "Abolishing Nuclear Armories: Policy or Pipedream?" *Survival* 49, no. 4 (Winter 2007–2008): 7–15.

16. Schell, *Seventh Decade,* p. 220.

17. 22 *U.S. Code,* 68a (Threat Reduction Cooperation with States of the Former Soviet Union).

18. Matthew Bunn, *Securing the Bomb 2007* (Cambridge, MA: Belfer Center for Science and International Affairs, John F. Kennedy School of Government, 2007); quotes are from the "Executive Summary," pp. v–xv.

19. IPCC, "Summary for Policymakers," in *Impacts, Adaptation, and Vulnerability: Contribution of Working Group II to the Fourth Assessment Report of the Intergovernmental Panel on Climate Change* (Cambridge: Cambridge University Press, 2007).

20. Similar consequences for regional and world order resulting from insufficient and sluggish responses to global warming were forecast by Kurt M. Cambell, Jay Gulledge, J. R. McNeill, John Podesta, Peter Ogden, Leon Feurth, R. James Woolsey, Alexander T. J. Lennon, Julianne Smith, Richard Weitz, and Derek Mix in *The Age of Consequences: The Foreign Policy and National Security Implications of Global Climate Change* (Washington, DC: Center for Strategic and International Studies/Center for a New American Security,

2007). See also the consensus report of eleven retired generals and admirals titled *National Security and the Threat of Climate Change*, published by the CNA Corporation in 2007 and available at SecurityAndClimate.cna.org, accessed on June 25, 2008.

21. Her Majesty's Treasury, "Summary of Conclusions," *Stern Review Report on the Economics of Climate Change* (October 2006), available at www.hm-treasury.gov.uk/independent_reviews/stern_review, accessed on December 15, 2007.

22. Ibid.

Notes for Chapter Four

1. George W. Bush, *The National Security Strategy of the United States* (Washington, DC: White House, September 20, 2002).

2. This section draws on my analysis of the Just War tradition in Seyom Brown, *The Illusion of Control: Force and Foreign Policy in the Twenty-first Century* (Washington, DC: Brookings Institution, 2003), pp. 105–141.

3. James Turner Johnson, *Morality and Contemporary Warfare* (New Haven, CT: Yale University Press, 1999).

4. Michael Walzer, *Just and Unjust Wars: A Moral Argument with Historical Illustrations* (New York: Basic Books, 1977), pp. 89–90.

5. I have adapted these Just War criteria from the 2004 report of the UN High-Level Panel on Threats, Challenges, and Change, *A More Secure World: Our Shared Responsibility*, UN Document A/59/565.

6. See chapter 3, note 3.

7. See Kenneth Waltz's arguments in Scott D. Sagan and Kenneth W. Waltz, *The Spread of Nuclear Weapons: A Debate Renewed* (New York: Norton, 2003).

8. *U.S. Strategic Bombing Survey, Overall Report* (Washington, DC: Government Printing Office, 1945).

9. See Lawrence Freedman, *The Revolution in Strategic Affairs*, Adelphi Paper 318 (London: International Institute for Strategic Studies, 1998), and Bruce Berkowitz, *The New Face of War: How War Will Be Fought in the 21st Century* (New York: Free Press, 2003).

10. Michael O'Hanlon, "Resurrecting the Test-Ban Treaty," *Survival* 50, no. 1 (February–March 2008): 119–132.

11. Richard F. Grimmett, *Congressional Research Service Report for Congress: Conventional Arms Transfers to Developing Nations 1999–2006* (Washington, DC: Congressional Research Service, September 26, 2007).

12. Graham Allison and Philip Zelikow, *The Essence of Decision: Explaining the Cuban Missile Crisis* (New York: Longman, 1999).

13. The importance of empathy was stressed by Roger Fisher and William Langer Ury in *Getting to Yes: Negotiating Agreement without Giving In* (Boston: Houghton Mifflin, 1981).

14. Henry Kissinger's utilization of the linkage approach in his step-by-step Middle Eastern diplomacy was described in Kissinger, *The White House Years* (Boston: Little, Brown, 1979), pp. 129–130.

15. For the Clinton administration's negotiations with North Korea, see Joel S. Wit, Daniel B. Poneman, and Robert L. Gallucci, *Going Critical: The First North Korean Nuclear Crisis* (Washington, DC: Brookings Institution, 2004).

16. Commenting on (but not really relieving) the terminological confusion, the UN High-Level Panel on Threats, Challenges, and Change reported to the secretary-general in December 2004 that "discussion of the necessary capacities has been confused by the tendency to refer to peacekeeping missions as 'Chapter VI operations' and peace enforcement missions as 'Chapter VII operations'—meaning consent-based or coercion-based, respectively. This shorthand is also often used to distinguish missions that do not involve the use of deadly force for purposes other than self-defense, and those that do." See UN High-Level Panel, *A More Secure World*, paragraph 211.

17. International Commission on Intervention and State Sovereignty, *Report: The Responsibility to Protect* (Ottawa: International Development Research Center, 2001). In its 2005 "World Summit," the UN General Assembly, in endorsing an international obligation to protect people from extreme maltreatment, specified that if national authorities are "manifestly failing to protect their populations from genocide, war crimes, ethnic cleansing, and crimes against humanity," Chapter VII operations (which could include the use of force) might be warranted. But for all other cases, the General Assembly resolution restricted the international response to peaceful means. See UN General Assembly Resolution A/RES/60/1.

18. These statistics were compiled in March 2008 from data issued by the UN Department of Peacekeeping Operations and the International Institute for Strategic Studies.

Notes for Chapter Five

1. UN Millennium Declaration, UN General Assembly Resolution A/res/55/2 (September 8, 2000).

2. Ban Ki-Moon, "Foreword," *Millennium Development Goals Report 2007* (New York: United Nations, 2007), p. 3.

3. The numerical estimates in this section are taken from the *Millennium Development Goals Report 2007.*

4. William Easterly, *The White Man's Burden: Why the West's Efforts to Aid the Rest Have Done So Much Ill and So Little Good* (New York: Penguin, 2006).

5. Jeffrey D. Sachs, *Common Wealth: Economics for a Crowded Planet* (New York: Penguin, 2008).

6. Another thoughtful contribution to these debates is provided by Paul Collier, in *The Bottom Billion: Why the Poorest Countries Are Failing and What Can Be Done about It* (New York: Oxford University Press, 2007).

7. Sachs, *Common Wealth*, pp. 298–300.

8. Paul Krugman, "Running Out of Planet to Exploit," *New York Times*, April 21, 2008.

9. "The New Face of Hunger," *Economist* 387, no. 8576 (April 19–25, 2008): 32–34.

10. Weldeghaber Kidhane, Materne Maetz, and Philippe Dardel, *Food Security and Agricultural Development in Sub-Saharan Africa: Building the Case for More Public Support* (Rome: Food and Agricultural Organization, 2006), p. 63.

11. Remarks of the El Salvadoran president at the World Economic Forum on Latin America, April 16, 2008, quoted in Marc Lacey, "Across Globe, Empty Bellies Bring Rising Anger," *New York Times*, April 18, 2008.

12. Sachs, *Common Wealth*, pp. 300–302.

13. The commons-user fee proposal can be thought of as a variation on the proposal by the Nobel laureate economist James Tobin for an international tax on cross-border currency transactions. The so-called Tobin Tax should also be given fresh consideration as a scheme for raising development funds for poor countries.

14. Easterly, *White Man's Burden*, p. 369.

15. José Antonio Ocampo (UN undersecretary-general for economic and social affairs), "Overview: Progress at the MDG Midpoint," *Millennium Development Goals Report 2007*, p. 5.

16. International Monetary Fund, *World Economic Outlook, October 2007: Globalization and Inequality* (Washington, DC: IMF, 2007).

Notes for Chapter Six

1. Joseph E. Stiglitz, *Globalization and Its Discontents* (New York: Norton, 2002), pp. 55–57.

2. Ibid., pp. 59–60.

3. International Monetary Fund, *World Economic Outlook: Globalization and Inequality* (Washington, DC: IMF, 2007).

4. William Overholt, "Exposing the Myths," RAND Corporation, available at www.rand/org/commentary/111703SCMP, accessed on June 2, 2008.

5. Direct access to credit from private international banks—another expression of globalization and of one's economic condition—tends to favor persons with higher incomes; this is particularly true where institutions are weak, for in such situations, only the wealthy, educated, and mobile elements of the population have such access. In turn, this increases inequality (unless the banks are involved in microfinance projects). See Eswar Prasad, Kenneth Rogoff, Shan-Jin Wei, and Ayhan Kose, "Financial Globalization, Growth, and Volatility in Developing Countries," in Ann Harrison, ed., *Globalization and Poverty* (Chicago: University of Chicago Press, 2007), pp. 457–516. As put by the authors of the IMF report, "A disproportionately larger share of financial flows accrues to those with higher endowments and income that can serve as collateral. As a result, the already better-off segments of the population are better able to invest in human and physical capital and increase their income." See IMF, *World Economic Outlook*, p. 157.

6. See Nancy Birdsall, "The World Is Not Flat: Inequality and Injustice in Our Global Economy," Lecture 9 (Helsinki: World Institute for Development Economics Research, 2005).

7. IMF, *World Economic Outlook*, pp. 157–158.

Notes for Chapter Seven

1. See Thomas F. Homer-Dixon, *Environment, Scarcity, and Violence* (Princeton, NJ: Princeton University Press, 1999).

2. UNEP, *Global Environmental Outlook (GEO-4): Summary for Decision Makers* (Valletta, Malta: UN Environmental Program, 2007).

3. UN Secretariat, Inter-agency and Expert Group on MDG Indicators, *Millennium Development Goals Report 2007* (New York: United Nations, 2007), p. 23.

4. Biologist Edward O. Wilson, who has done more than any other scientist to alert the world to the alarming loss of biodiversity, attributes the phenomenon to five assaults on the planet's ecosystems: habitat destruction, invasive species, pollution, population increase, and overharvesting—all of which are potentially reversible by concerted policy initiatives. See Wilson, *The Creation: An Appeal to Save Life on Earth* (New York: Norton, 2006).

5. UNEP, Millennium Ecosystem Assessment, *Ecosystems and Human Well-Being: Biodiversity Synthesis* (Washington, DC: World Resources Institute, Island Press, 2005).

6. For the politics of the ozone-layer depletion issue, see Richard Elliot Benedick, *Ozone Diplomacy: New Directions in Safeguarding the Planet* (Cambridge, MA: Harvard University Press, 1991). See also Pamela S. Chasek, David L. Downie, and Janet Welsh Brown, *Global Environmental Politics* (Boulder, CO: Westview, 2006), pp. 106–115.

7. The geostationary orbit congestion problem was foreseen by Seyom Brown, Nina W. Cornell, Larry L. Fabian, and Edith Brown Weiss in their *Regimes for the Ocean, Outer Space, and Weather* (Washington, DC: Brookings Institution, 1977), pp. 178–180, 201.

8. Robin McKie and Michael Day, "Warning of Catastrophe from Mass of 'Space Junk,'" *Observer*, February 24, 2008; Kelly Young, "Anti-satellite Test Generates Dangerous Space Debris," *New Scientist* (January 2007), available at www.space.newscientist.com, accessed on July 1, 2008.

9. World Commission on Environment and Development, *Our Common Future* (New York: Oxford University Press, 1987), pp. 27, 38.

10. The classic "Tragedy of the [British] Commons," analyzed by Garret Hardin in *Science* 162 (December 3, 1968): 1234–1248, is not something we should want to emulate, either in its origins or in its "solution."

11. Seyom Brown et al., *Regimes for the Ocean, Outer Space, and Weather.*

Notes for Chapter Eight

1. Statement of Secretary of State Madeleine K. Albright before the Senate Finance Committee, June 10, 1977. Quoted in Seyom Brown, *Human Rights in World Politics* (New York: Longman, 2000), pp. 129–130.

2. U.S. Department of State, *Country Reports on Human Rights Practices for [year]* (Washington, DC: Government Printing Office, issued annually). These reports are submitted each year to the House of Representatives Committee on International Relations and to the Senate Foreign Relations Committee. They are also publicly released and available at www.state.gov.

3. The basic legislative stipulations denying foreign assistance to governments that are found to engage in gross violations of human rights appear in the *Foreign Assistance Act of 1974* and the *Arms Export Control Act of 1976.*

4. Bruce Russett, *Grasping the Democratic Peace* (Princeton, NJ: Princeton University Press, 1993); John Owen, "Give Democratic Peace a Chance: How Liberalism Produces Democratic Peace," *International Security* 19, no. 2 (Autumn 1994): 87–125; and Michael E. Brown, Sean M. Lynn-Jones, and Steven E. Miller, *Debating the Democratic Peace* (Cambridge, MA: MIT Press, 1996).

5. Edward D. Mansfield and Jack Snyder, "Democratic Transitions, Institutional Strength, and War," *International Organization* 56, no. 2 (Spring 2002): 297–337; Jack Snyder, *From Voting to Violence: Democratization and Violent Conflict* (New York: Norton, 2000); and Edward D. Mansfield and Jack Snyder, *Electing to Fight: Why Emerging Democracies Go to War* (Cambridge: Massachusetts Institute of Technology Press, 2005).

6. Thomas Carothers, "Responding to the Democracy Promotion Backlash," testimony before the Senate Foreign Relations Committee, June 8, 2006, available at www.carnegieendowment.org/publications.

7. Paul Collier, *The Bottom Billion: Why the Poorest Countries Are Failing and What Can Be Done About It* (New York: Oxford University Press, 2007).

8. Morton H. Halperin, Joseph T. Siegle, and Michael M. Weinstein, *The Democracy Advantage: How Democracies Promote Prosperity and Peace* (New York: Routledge, 2005).

9. Secretary of State Vance's guidelines were the product of an interagency process chaired by Deputy Secretary of State Warren Christopher, and they were issued to all agencies and U.S. embassies abroad as the Carter administration's authoritative statement on human rights issues. The secretary revealed these guidelines to the public in an address at the University of Georgia Law School on April 30, 1977, which was published in the *Department of State Bulletin*, May 23, 1977, pp. 505–508.

10. International Commission on Intervention and State Sovereignty, *The Responsibility to Protect: Report of the International Commission on Intervention and State Sovereignty* (Ottawa: International Development Research Center, 2001). See also United Nations, *2005 World Summit Outcome*, UN General Assembly Document A/60L.1, December 15, 2005.

11. Michael Walzer, *Thick and Thin: Moral Argument at Home and Abroad* (Notre Dame, IN: University of Notre Dame Press, 1994).

Notes for Chapter Nine

1. Samuel P. Huntington, *The Clash of Civilizations and the Remaking of World Order* (New York: Simon and Schuster, 1996).

2. Nazith Ayubi, *Political Islam: Religion and Politics in the Arab World* (New York: Routledge, 1991).

3. An authoritative translation is found in *Koran* (London: Penguin Classics, 1956).

4. On the manifold versions and applications of sharia, see Noah Feldman, "Why Shariah?" *New York Times Magazine*, March 16, 2008.

5. Bernard Lewis, *The Political Language of Islam* (Chicago: University of Chicago Press, 1988). See also Ann Elizabeth Mayer, *Islam and Human Rights: Tradition and Politics* (Boulder, CO: Westview, 1999).

6. S. Radhakrishnan, *The Hindu View of Life* (London: Allen and Unwin, 1954), p. 107.

7. Louis Henkin, "The Human Rights Idea in China: A Comparative Perspective," in R. Randall Edwards, Louis Henkin, and Andrew J. Nathan, eds., *Human Rights in Contemporary China* (New York: Columbia University Press, 1986).

8. *Analects of Confucius*, 12:19, in Wing-Tsit Chan, *A Source Book in Chinese Philosophy* (Princeton, NJ: Princeton University Press, 1993), p. 40.

9. Chan, *Source Book*, p. 131.

10. Bilahari Kausikan, "Asia's Different Standard," *Foreign Policy* 92 (Fall 1993): 24–41, quote from 35–36.

11. Amartya Sen, *Identity and Violence: The Illusion of Destiny* (New York: Norton, 2006), and Kwame Anthony Appiah, *Cosmopolitanism: Ethics in a World of Strangers* (New York: Norton, 2006).

12. Will Kymlicka, *Multicultural Odysseys: Navigating the New International Politics of Diversity* (New York: Oxford University Press, 2007).

Notes for Chapter Ten

1. For a conceptual scholarly analysis of the various means (and difficulty) of enhancing transnational accountability processes and institutions, see Ruth W. Grant and Robert O. Keohane, "Accountability and the Abuses of Power in World Politics," *American Political Science Review* 99, no. 1 (February 2005): 29–43.

2. See typical proposals for reforming the membership and voting rules of the Security Council in *A More Secure World: Our Shared Responsibility*, 2004 Report of the UN High-Level Panel on Threat, Challenges, and Change, UN Document A/59/565, especially pp. 66–69.

3. *American Interests and UN Reform*. Report of a task force organized by the United States Institute of Peace (Washington: United States Institute of Peace, December 2005).

4. *Treaty on the Non-proliferation of Nuclear Weapons (NPT)*, Articles I and II, International Atomic Energy Agency Document INFCIRC/140, April 22, 1970.

5. Ibid., Articles III, IV, V, and VI.

6. Negotiations for implementing the Kyoto Protocol to the UN Framework Convention on Climate Change are described in Pamela S. Chasek, David L. Downie,

and Janet Welsh Brown, *Global Environmental Politics* (Boulder, CO: Westview, 2006), pp. 122–128.

7. See the discussion in chapter 7 for an analysis of the costs of abating global warming versus the costs of dealing with its consequences.

8. The Concert of Democracies was one of the principal recommendations made in the report of the Princeton Project on National Security, *Forging a World of Liberty under Law: U.S. National Security in the Twenty-first Century* (Princeton, NJ: Princeton University Woodrow Wilson School of Public Affairs, 2006), p. 7.

9. Kishore Mahbubani, "Charting a New Course," *Survival* 49, no. 3 (Autumn 2007): 207.

Notes for Chapter Eleven

1. David Rothkopf, *Running the World: The Inside Story of the National Security Council and the Architects of American Power* (New York: Public Affairs, 2005). For the extent to which the bureaucratic politics tail can wag the foreign policy dog, see Morton H. Halperin, with Pricilla Clapp and Arnold Kanter, *Bureaucratic Politics and Foreign Policy* (Washington, DC: Brookings Institution, 1974).

2. Graham Allison and Philip Zelikow, *Essence of Decision: Explaining the Cuban Missile Crisis,* 2nd ed. (New York: Longman, 1999).

3. Irving Janis, *Groupthink: Psychological Studies of Policy Decisions and Fiascos* (Boston: Houghton Mifflin, 1982).

4. See Bob Woodward's accounts, *Plan of Attack* (New York: Simon and Schuster, 2004), and *State of Denial* (New York: Simon and Schuster, 2006).

Notes for Chapter Twelve

1. George P. Shultz, William J. Perry, Henry A. Kissinger, and Sam Nunn, "A World Free of Nuclear Weapons," *Wall Street Journal,* January 4, 2007. See my discussion of this initiative in chapter 3.

2. Program on International Policy Attitudes [hereafter referred to as PIPA], *Americans and Russians in Nuclear Weapons and the Future of Disarmament* (College Park: University of Maryland, November 9, 2007), a joint study of World Public Opinion .org and the Advanced Methods of Cooperative Security Program of the Center for International and Security Studies at Maryland (CISSM), p. 16.

3. Ibid., p. 6.

4. Ibid., p. 9.

5. Ibid., p. 4.

6. Ibid., p. 7.

7. PIPA/Knowledge Networks Poll, *Americans on Climate Change: 2005* (College Park: University of Maryland, July 5, 2005).

8. *Newsweek*/Princeton Survey Research Associates International Poll, August 1–2, 2007, available at www.thedailybackground.com/category/polls.

9. Again, the most useful and reliable reporting on the surveys (of their own and other polling organizations) is provided by the PIPA operation. Its comprehensive report entitled *Americans on Foreign Aid and World Hunger: A Study of U.S. Public Attitudes* was published in 2001, and its major findings still hold.

10. Ibid.

11. WorldPublicOpinion.org, *Global Issue—United Nations,* available at www.american-world.org/digest/global_issues/un, accessed April 9, 2008.

12. See the various polls by the Chicago Council on Foreign Relations on attitudes toward U.S. participation in the International Criminal Court, cited in ibid.

Notes for Conclusion

1. Niall Fuerguson, "A World without Power," *Foreign Policy* 143 (July–August 2004): 32–39.

2. Richard N. Haass, "The Age of Nonpolarity: What Will Follow US Dominance?" *Foreign Affairs* 87, no. 3 (May–June 2008).

3. Remarks by Stephen Hadley at the Kennedy Center, Washington, DC, June 5, 2008, available at www.whitehouse.gov/news/releases/2008/06, accessed on July 5, 2008.

4. Secretary of Defense Robert M. Gates, Landon Lecture at Kansas State University, November 25, 2007, available at www.defenselink.mil/speeches/speech.aspx?speechchid=1199. See also the Pentagon's June 2008 issuance of its *National Defense Strategy* under the signature of Secretary Gates (Washington, DC: Department of Defense, 2008), accessed on INSIDEDEFENSE.COM, on August 1, 2008.

5. Condoleezza Rice, "Rethinking the National Interest: American Realism for a New World," *Foreign Affairs* 87, no. 4 (July–August 2008): 2–26.

Index

About the Author

Seyom Brown is the John Goodwin Tower Distinguished Chair in International Politics and National Security in the Department of Political Science at Southern Methodist University, and Director of Studies at the Tower Center for Political Studies. He is also a Senior Advisor to the Security Studies Program at the Massachusetts Institute of Technology. Before coming to SMU, Dr. Brown was the Lawrence A. Wien Professor of International Cooperation at Brandeis University and a Senior Fellow in the Belfer Center for Science and International Affairs at the John F. Kennedy School of Government, Harvard University.

He has held senior research and policy analysis positions at the RAND Corporation, the Brookings Institution, and the Carnegie Endowment for International Peace, and has served as a Special Assistant in the Office of International Security Affairs in the Department of Defense and a Special Assistant to the Director of Policy Planning in the Department of State. In addition to *Higher Realism,* Dr. Brown is the author of eleven books on U.S. foreign policy and international relations, including *The Illusion of Control: Force and Foreign Policy in the 21st Century; The Faces of Power: Constancy and Change in United States Foreign Policy from Truman to Clinton; International Relations in a Changing Global System; Human Rights in World Politics; The Causes and Prevention of War;* and *New Forces, Old Forces, and the Future of World Politics.*